The Far Western Frontier

The Far Western Frontier

Advisory Editor

RAY A. BILLINGTON

Senior Research Associate
at the Henry E. Huntington Library
and Art Gallery

THE

Experiences of a Forty-niner

IN

CALIFORNIA

BY
CHARLES D. FERGUSON

EDITED BY
FREDERICK T. WALLACE

ARNO PRESS
A NEW YORK TIMES COMPANY
New York • 1973

Reprint Edition 1973 by Arno Press Inc.

Reprinted from a copy in The State
Historical Society of Wisconsin Library

The Far Western Frontier
ISBN for complete set: 0-405-04955-2
See last pages of this volume for titles.

Manufactured in the United States of America

Publisher's Note: This book was originally
published as The Experiences of a Forty-niner
During Thirty-four Years' Residence in California
and Australia. Cleveland, 1888.

Library of Congress Cataloging in Publication Data

Ferguson, Charles D   b. 1832 or 3.
    The experiences of a Forty-Niner in California.

    (The Far Western frontier)
    Reprint of the 1888 ed.
    1. The West--Description and travel--1848-1860.
2. California--Gold discoveries. 3. Overland
journeys to the Pacific. I. Title. II. Series.
F593.F37 1973   917.94   72-9442
ISBN 0-405-04971-4

87628

I—On the Way to the Mines in 1849.   II—A Scene in Camp.   III—Landing Three
Miles Below Sacramento City.   IV.—Sutter's Famous Adobe Fort in 1849.

[By courtesy of The Magazine of American History.]

CHARLES D. FERGUSON.

1853.

CHARLES D. FERGUSON.
1887.

THE

Experiences of a Forty-niner

IN

CALIFORNIA

BY
CHARLES D. FERGUSON

EDITED BY
FREDERICK T. WALLACE

INTRODUCTORY.

IT is a suggestive if not a significant coincidence, that the Hebrew historian of creation assigned to man a primitive abode in the now unknown Eden, watered in part by the lost Pison, embracing within its area the "land of Havilah, where there is gold," and making assurance doubly sure of the excellency of the mineral products of that country in the statement that "the gold of that land is good," besides abounding in bdellium and the onyx stone.

Gold, as the most precious and most highly prized of minerals, wrought into articles of personal adornment, coronal emblems of royalty, or as a medium in the commerce of nations, is prehistoric. The tombs of Egypt are now surrendering golden treasures and exquisite personal ornaments that once adorned the daughters of Pharaoh and the ladies of the Egyptian court, thousands of years before the golden calf was set up and worshiped in the valley before Sinai. The passion for the acquisition of gold is an inheritance from our remote ancestry of Havilah, surpassing in intensity the desire for any other mineral known to man. Gold is a familiar word, pervading all written history, sacred and profane; employed alike

III

by prophet, priest and king. And throughout sacred liter-
ature gold is the emblem of purity, and refined gold the
standard of comparison with faith, hope and love.

When the author of Genesis wrote, the geographical
locality of Havilah was doubtless well known to him and
his readers, and was the source from which came the gold
of prehistoric antiquity. Since the Havilah gold fields
were worked, three great epochs of gold discovery have
passed, each leaving its impress upon nations, states and
social life. Like the course of empire, gold discoveries
have been westward, until the circuit of the earth has been
compassed. Neither in the Scriptures nor in the histories
of the monarchies of the Euphrates, do we get but occasionally a faint glimpse of the industries of the people
or the commercial character of the ancient nations; but
all relates to the wars of rival sovereigns and religious
ceremonies, and but for the brief allusion to the building
of ships at Ezion-geber, by Solomon, which made three
years' voyages to the unknown Ophir and returned
freighted with gold, sandal-wood and peacocks, one would
suppose his splendid reign consisted mainly in building a
temple and writing songs. Nevertheless, his reign was
manifestly one of great commercial enterprise. He was
the first truly historical discoverer of a new gold field. It
resulted in vast wealth to his empire and a royal fame
which has come down to us surpassing that of all other
oriental monarchs, the glories of which astonished the
queen of Sheba, past whose royal dominions his ships
had sailed out of the Red sea into mysterious waters, and
returned laden with the wealth of Ormuz and of Ind. Jeru-

salem suddenly rose from an interior mountain village to a city of the first class, ranking with Tyre and Sidon and Damascus. With the gold of Ophir he built Tadmor in the wilderness, embellished the city, built the walls thereof, Millo, and a palace for his Egyptian wife, the daughter of Pharaoh.

Such as remember the news by the ship from "around the Horn," now just forty years ago, will not need to draw wholly upon their imagination for the effect produced by the return of the Ophir fleet, how Tyre and Sidon and the cities of Asia Minor, from Tarsus to Ephesus and Troy, were agitated by the news, how the lumbermen of Mount Lebanon and the artisans of Damascus were stricken with the Ophir fever, and were carried away in the next fleet that sailed.

Twenty-five hundred years later and two thousand miles further to the westward, in Spain, when the western ocean had relaxed its chains and a vast continent had appeared with cities, states and empires unheard of before Columbus—of an antiquity coeval with Egypt—Pizarro sent home to his sovereign millions in gold—spoils of the plundered Temple of the Sun in the empire of the Inca of Peru. Then from the Pillars of Hercules to the Pyrenees, and from the Tagus to the Ebro, the gold fever raged to a degree then unprecedented in history, resulting in voluntary emigration such as no other country ever experienced. the acquisition of a continent, and two hundred years of colonization, national prestige and sovereign grandeur. Finally the defeat of the Duke of Medina Sidonia and the destruction of the "invincible" Armada—loss of prestige and of provinces, culminating in national decay. For more than two hundred years Peruvian gold, transported in the galleons of Spain, furnished the incentive to piracy and freebooting, so long the terror of the seas.

The passion for gold of the government of Spain and the higher ranks of its subjects was so intense as to eventuate in crimes and cruelties more terrible than ever before were perpetrated by civilized man upon a gentle and inoffensive people. Emigration from Spain to Mexico and Peru from 1492 for more than a hundred years, far surpassed that of England for the colonization of North America from 1607 for an equal length of time—the one inspired by gold, the other by liberty of conscience and the spirit of freedom.

But it was reserved to the middle of the nineteenth century to record the most wonderful discoveries of gold in the history of the human race. With California and Australia so recent and familiar to all, the record of discovery would seem to be forever closed. These two simultaneous events not only deeply affected the commercial and social institutions of America and Europe, but brought into existence great states and an ocean empire whose places on the map of the world theretofore had been designated only as territory unexplored.

It is yet within the memory of the middle-aged how intensely the country was agitated, when, in 1848, the news came of the discovery of gold in California. Not even the late civil war occupied the public mind more than did the golden regions of the Pacific coast for several years. Emigration thereto instantly set in, each individual inspired by hopes of acquisition of a portion of the rich deposits, which for multitude was beyond comprehension and almost beyond belief. It is doubtful if there was a city, village or rural town in the United States that was unrepresented in California or Australia during the first five years of the golden age of those countries.

Of the vast multitude who sought those lands hundreds and probably thousands never reached them, but whose unknown graves dot the plains, whose bones lie scattered upon the deserts, or rest among the coral reefs of the Pacific ocean. The spirit of adventure pervaded old and young alike, and the gray-haired man and the beardless boy were partners and companions in that most hazardous enterprise of the age.

In this volume is sought to be recorded something of the personal experiences during a third of a century of one among the thousands of Ohio boys who were "out in the forty-nine." The pleasant town of Aurora was his home. He has related in the following narrative his youthful aspirations and the circumstances attending his departure. The editor assumes the responsibility of an allusion to him personally, and to his ancestry very briefly, that the reader of his narrative may be confirmed in the truth of the saying that "blood will tell." In the battle of Culloden, where "Proud Cumberland prances, insulting the slain," his Scotch great-grandfather fell. The son of the ancient hero, John Ferguson, at the age of sixteen years became a voluntary exile in France, and came to America with Lafayette, served through the Revolution, was captain of a company, and at the close of the war settled in Blandford, Massachusetts. His son, Samuel H. Ferguson, at the age of twenty came to Ohio and settled in Aurora, where he married Julia Forward, daughter of Judge Forward who settled there in 1803, and sister of Honorable Walter Forward, secretary of the treasury of the United States, in the cabinet of President Harrison. She dying, he subsequently married Anna McKinney, a widowed lady, whose mother was Anna Holly of Litchfield, Connecticut, and sister of Honorable John Mattocks, one of the early senators of the United States, for that state. Mr. Charles D. Ferguson, whose experiences are related in this volume, is the son of Samuel H. Ferguson by his second marriage. He is still, at the age of fifty-five years, a gentleman of restless activity, energy of character and high spirit, and the reader will not fail to discover in the following pages something of his mental capacity, Scottish prudence and intelligent foresight, blended with and supplemented by the bravery and gallant bearing of a Roderick Dhu.

In the preparation of the pages of this book the editor has had the benefit of very ample notes, recently made by the narrator from memory, he never having kept a written diary, and of many personal interviews. In yielding to the importunities of many to put a few of his experiences into readable form, he has constantly insisted that no exaggerations shall be indulged in, and nothing stated but the simple truth.

As all or nearly all of the events and incidents relate to matters personal to himself or within his own observation, the editor has deemed it but natural and proper that the narrative should take the form of the first person. And now without apology, excuse or further explanation the reader is respectfully referred to the narrative of one whose experiences for a third of a century have been, to say the least, remarkable, if not unprecedented, in individual history since Marco Polo, at the age of seventeen, left his palatial home in Venice, traversed the continent of Asia, passed over the Himalaya mountains and crossed the desert of Gobi, to the court and empire of Kublai Khan, now just six hundred years ago.

F. T. WALLACE.

CLEVELAND, January, 1888.

CONTENTS.

XI

ILLUSTRATIONS.

CHAPTER I.

AMONG the many thousands who, in 1848, were excited to the verge of lunacy on the arrival of the news from "around the Horn," announcing the discovery of gold by Marshall, at Sutter's mill, on American river, California, the relater of the events and experiences recorded in this book was one. Visions of gold excited my brain. It was not the gold alone, but an awakening of a strong desire of adventure which had pervaded my spirit from a small school-boy taking my first lesson in geography. Foreign countries marked upon the pages of the little school atlas were fascinating, and many were the pictures I drew in my youthful imagination of some future time when, by travel, I should know more of the world. How I did envy Captain Cook and Robinson Crusoe, the latter especially. I remember one day resting with my brother under the shade of a tree near our old Ohio homestead when a sedate gentleman rode by on horseback. "Do you know that man?" said my brother. I said no. "That is Judge Eben Newton," said my brother, "and he is what I will be some day. What will you be?" asked my brother. "I will be a traveler," said I, "and see the world." It is a strange coincidence that the two lads under the shade tree reached, respectively, the height of his boyish ambition—I to my heart's content.

There were numerous other boys in our neighborhood who had the gold fever, caught, doubtless, in some instances, from me, for it was surely "catching." Many were the evenings we got together and laid our plans. There was not a newspaper that had an item about gold that was not learned by heart, and great pains taken to enlarge and embellish the accounts to our parents. When I succeeded in getting my dear old father's and mother's consent to let me go, I was the proudest boy in Ohio. Pictures of untold wealth nearly drove me wild. This, however, was but for a short period, for, as the time drew near for my departure, my parents suddenly changed their minds. I was too young, they said, to go out into the world of temptations, and especially among the Indians. My heart sank ten degrees below zero, but it was of no use; the old people had settled it, and go I should not. But to conciliate my wounded spirit and recompense me for my disappointment, they agreed that I might go and visit Doctor George W. McKinney, a half-brother, living at Ottawa, Illinois. I grasped the situation. Now was my chance, and I was determined not to throw it away. I appeared to be satisfied with the arrangement and soon left home, little thinking that thirty-four years would pass away

before I should return, and then to find that other hands
than mine had to assist in laying my aged and gray-haired
parents in their quiet rural graves, and that, too, many
long years before their seemingly thoughtless but not un-
feeling son returned. O, how many sleepless nights, how
many anxious hours they have waited and waited for my
return! My dear old mother's dying words were: "Tell
Charles I have waited and waited until I can wait no
longer, and only hope to meet him in Heaven." Heaven
rest her soul. May her joys surpass the sorrows I caused
her here upon earth.

It was in the month of September, 1849, when, at the
age of seventeen years, I bade good-by to father, mother
and friends, and repaired to Cleveland where I embarked
on the lake steamer *A. D. Patchen* for Chicago. It was
late in the season, the weather generally rough, and my
trip was not an exception, unless it was unusually rough,
which I think it was, since I have experienced many severe
storms on the ocean hardly more severe. Had I been on
shore, and safe at home, I would have been content to remain there and let gold-seeking go to David Jones' locker.
But that feeling soon vanished after arriving at Chicago.
It was, however, not the Chicago of to-day, for I think the
population did not exceed seventeen thousand. Among
the incidents of this lake voyage was one on Lake Huron.
There were many clergymen passengers on board who
were on their return from a conference at Buffalo. In the
midst of the storm Captain Whitaker passed through the
saloon in a great hurry, when the ministers accosted him
to know if there was any danger? "Danger! Yes, we will

all be in h—l together in less than ten minutes!" The ministers united in both audible and silent prayer till the storm abated. A passenger came aboard at some port near the head of Lake Michigan. He had been left by some other boat the day before. He was intoxicated, and after supper walked out on the hurricane deck and fell overboard. The engine was stopped and boats lowered, but to no purpose; the poor fellow had sunk to rise no more, unless at the final resurrection. His wife came aboard at Chicago to look for him. But, alas, no husband was there, and the only memento she obtained was his hat. Thus ended my first voyage on the inland seas.

From Chicago to Ottawa, eighty miles by canal, took twenty-four hours, which is now accomplished by rail in less than three. At Ottawa I found the gold excitement as intense, if not more so, than in Ohio; so there was no hope for my recovery from the fever, since I had already relapsed from the first attack, and doctors say a relapse is more liable to be fatal than the first attack. I found it so in my case. There is no disease or desire on earth so contagious as the gold fever. There is no asylum for the patient and no physician who can minister to a mind thus diseased.

My mind was made up to go to California and nothing but death could stop me. But how to get away was the only thing that troubled me. I had spent my money rather freely among my brother's friends, to whom in a short time I had become quite warmly attached, and who in compliment to my cheerful intercourse with them, unanimously voted me a "chip of the old block," however that may be interpreted. Most of them are dead now (1887). A few remain in Ottawa. Arthur Lockwood is still there. William Earle now lives at La Salle, Colorado, I believe, though I have not seen him since my return to this country. Doctor Thomas, another of my early Ottawa friends, lives in Samanock, La Salle county, Illinois, and whom I recently had the pleasure of visiting. Others, if they still live, are scattered and distributed among the great states of the west, and whom I shall never probably meet again on earth.

How to approach my brother on the subject of going to California was a perplexing matter to me. Soon, however, a favorable moment came. Winter had nearly gone, and spring was approaching with all its suggestiveness of activity and labor. One day my brother asked me what I intended to do. My courage failed me when put to the test. I answered, of course, that I did not know. He made me several offers, and suggested several fields of enterprise which almost any young man, in less excitable times, would have deemed advantageous and fortunate, but all of which I declined. My apparent indifference to his every suggestion doubtless seemed to him to indicate either stupidity or ingratitude, and he was justly provoked when he passionately said: "What in h—l do you want to do?" My brother's indignation inspired me with boldness. This was my opportunity, and I improved it by saying in the most frank and respectful manner possible, that I wanted to go to California. He made no reply, but called his wife and said to her: "This young man wants to go to California," and without waiting for her even to express her astonishment, he told her to pack my things and let me go. She pleaded with me for my mother's sake, but to no purpose. I was going now, and no mistake.

There were three others of Ottawa friends of Doctor Thomas and pleasant acquaintances of mine, who were making arrangements to go, and I entered into an agreement to join them. All things being ready, and considering delays dangerous, we were anxious to be off at once. So on the fourteenth of March, 1850, we left Ottawa for Peru, where we were to take steamer for St. Louis. We found a steamer about ready to run down the Illinois river. The captain of the *Ocean Wave*, for such was its imposing name, remembered, doubtless, by many even unto this day, agreed to take ourselves, four in number, four horses and a wagon to St. Louis, for the modest sum of twenty-four dollars. The only stop we made on our trip down the river of any considerable length of time was at Peoria, and I shall ever remember this place for the pleasant impressions it made upon my mind. Even at this early day it was quite imposing—a magnificent place. I had never seen then, nor have I since, a place where nature had been so lavish in her endowments to make a beautiful city. I have thought of it and spoken of it many times in foreign lands. as the loveliest little town I ever saw. We arrived in St. Louis on the eighteenth of March, where the *Ocean Wave* was made fast in her place and we disembarked. Here I was impressed with the vast number of steamers along the levee. It seemed to me they numbered thousands. For miles along the levee they lay three and four deep. The sugar and cotton steamers belonging to the lower Mississippi were readily distinguished from those of the upper Mississippi. The hands on board the former were all negroes. When night came they would all assemble around the capstan, and one would lead off in a song, the others would join in, the next boat's crew would take it up, and so on until the whole was one grand concert from one end of the levee to the other. Since then I have listened to fashionable operas, and heard renowned prima-donnas, but never have I heard the human voice utter such sweetness and melody as then and there came from the lips of the dusky boatmen of the Mississippi.

We placed our horses in a livery on Third street and took up our quarters at a hotel on the same street, the name of which I have forgotten. I only remember it was the best hotel then in St. Louis. I always have had a weakness that way when traveling to patronize the best, which I have always found cheapest in the end. Besides, if one puts up at a respectable house, he has the advantage of better associations, and many times, especially if he is a stranger, it may possibly lead him in the way of business, if, perchance, he may be a second Micawber, waiting for something to turn up. Our first necessity incident to the great, laborious and hazardous enterprise of traversing the almost unknown interior of the continent, its vast plains, great rivers, and dangerous and doubtful passes, and terrific cañons of the Rocky mountains, was to purchase a stock of provisions. This consisted chiefly of bacon, flour, hardtack, tea, coffee and sugar. Two quarts of No. 6 extract of cayenne pepper was deemed a necessity, as was also a gallon of the best brandy procurable. Each purchased a Colt's revolver with ample accompaniments for the special benefit of the Indians, and which we afterwards and on many occasions, found to be a very potent and influential Indian persuader.

Our next business was to look for a steamer bound for St. Joseph, some three hundred miles up the Missouri river. This was not a very difficult task, as there were many along the upper levee all ready to start, and each one offered the best advantages, and each was represented to arrive there in the shortest possible time. I may here remark that these river steamers had each its own particular route and river waters. Those which ply on the Illinois river do not run on the Mississippi, only to St. Louis, and the Missouri steamers come down only to the same city, and the great cotton and sugar transports and passenger boats of the lower Mississippi do not ply above the same point. It was somewhat difficult to decide upon a boat among so many and all holding out pleasant inducements, but we finally made our selection and paid our passage—six dollars each—which also covered the transportation of our horses, wagon, provisions and provender. It was the best and cheapest contract we could make, as we thought then, but the sequel failed to confirm our opinion.

CHAPTER II.

Steamer "Orient"—Passengers a Hard Lot—Thief Knocked Overboard—Complimented by the Captain—Independence and St. Joseph—Old Fort Kearney—First Camp—Drowned Out—Crossing the Missouri—Salt Creek, Now Lincoln, Nebraska—A Santa Fé Post Rider—Party of Pawnees—Deer Shooting—A Man with a Wheelbarrow.

WE were now treading the deck of the *Orient*. The charm of the name seemed to surpass that of the *Ocean Wave*, but when we got fairly under way, and even before we entered upon the long stretch of the Missouri, and took a survey of our numerous companions of the voyage, the romance and poetry suggested by the names of western river steamers vanished. I have traveled some since, but never have I fell in with such a congregation of self-conceited, ignorant, disagreeable and annoying lot of passengers as crowded the *Orient*. I do not believe another such lot ever got together. Others have related to me similar experiences, but not a single instance could hold a candle to this experience of my own.

I have always observed, when thrown among people that were ignorant, rough and mean, that they were jealous of those whom they considered better informed and better behaved and who were, in fact, their superiors. Such

will form cliques among themselves for the purpose of insulting or annoying you. It is on their part an uncon-
scious acknowledgment of your superiority. Such was the
class of passengers we had on board the steamer *Orient*.
To begin with, they were the worst set of petty thieves I
ever knew. They very early set to work to rob our four
Canadian ponies of their feed. Our bales of hay dimin-
ished rapidly and the mangers were robbed. At last I
caught one of them taking the hay from the ponies. I
remonstrated with him, but he only laughed and made fun
of me. The others gathered around and jeered and
laughed, told me to go home to my mother. I was told
by one to hold my tongue, or he would throw me overboard. My young blood was a little stirred at such a
threat, and I challenged him to try it, and sure enough he
collared me. He did not think of throwing me over, but
only to frighten me, expecting I would beg off, when they
would have the laugh on me. But he misjudged the Ohio
boy. We clinched, and struggling out by the aft gang-
way, near the wheel, it being a side-wheeler, I gave a sudden turn and loosed myself from him, and at the same
moment planted my fist full and fairly in his face with such
energy as my then unpracticed fighting muscle admitted
of, and he fell back and overboard. I confess I felt a little
frightened, but the water was not more than three feet
deep, and when I saw him standing on his feet in the middle of the river, my equanimity was fully restored. The
boat stopped, a skiff was lowered, and the man was soon
picked up and brought aboard. His nose was bleeding and
he was crestfallen. Knowing that such a class of men are

THE THIEF KNOCKED OVERBOARD.

invariably cowards, and that even a little swagger will command their respect, I therefore notified his friends who wished to take a bath to avail themselves of my services, then and there—adding that it was no unusual thing for me to throw a man or two overboard every morning, to give myself an appetite for breakfast. When the captain learned how matters stood, he told them if any more of them were caught stealing and got thrown overboard, he would not stop to pick them up. After this oration from the captain, he, turning to me, said: "Come on, youngster, with me and take a drink." I did not taste strong drink in those days, but I thanked the captain and respectfully declined his proffered civility. All this, however, had its influence. The ponies were no more robbed of their provender, and, as for my partners and myself, we were treated with civility during the remainder of the trip. It is a lamentably strange peculiarity of mind of this class of people that they will respect you only when they fear you. Trust them and deal gently and kindly with them, as one man should with another, and in return they will insult you, annoy you, and plunder you.

Our progress was rather slow, as the current of the Missouri changes almost daily, and it is impossible for a pilot to know the current from one day to another, and hence we were obliged to tie up every night. Our first stopping place for the discharge of passengers was at Independence, where the worst of the lot were let off, much to our comfort and relief. On our arrival at St. Joseph, we bade farewell to the *Orient* and the remainder of its uncompanionable emigrants. We were much disappointed at the appearance of this then famous town. It was talked about almost as much as St. Louis, both before and after we were on our way to it. Our ideas of its size and importance had been greatly exaggerated, but no one could tell us anything definite about it more than I could tell them, which was just nothing at all. It was, however, important in the sense of being the last frontier town on the east bank of the Missouri, in the northwest corner of the state. Old Fort Kearney, about one hundred miles up the river, and on its west bank, was the only name then known on the map. All the great interior passed under the general name of Nebraska. The great states and territories now familiar to us, carved from that vast region between the upper Missouri and the Rocky mountains, was but the home of the red man and the range of the buffalo. Most of the houses of St. Joseph were but little temporary huts. There were a very few passably good buildings. The population would not exceed seven hundred. There had been many arrivals before us, and all were waiting for the grass to grow before launching out upon the plains. Many did not attempt the journey until the first of May.

Our horses having been on board the *Orient* for several days, were as pleased as ourselves at once more getting on land, and were not long in showing it, for one of them, by some carelessness, got away and started out on his own account to take in the town. The other three seeing him enjoying such unwonted freedom, became suddenly inspired with the spirit of liberty and broke loose. St. Jo, as the place is always called, for short, suddenly advanced

PONIES TAKING IN ST. JO.

from a one-horse town to a four-horse city. The four Canadian ponies created more excitement than the town had ever before been wrought up to. Every man, woman and child were out to lend a hand in catching them, but all to no purpose; the ponies were going to have their time out—and they did. When they were through, all four deliberately walked into the nearest livery-stable and took their places in vacant stalls. I have often since thought it would be a good way to advertise horses, for the dealer to turn his whole stock loose in town and let them show themselves, for certainly no frontier town ever saw a grander sight than those four Canucks, with flowing manes, arched necks and expanded nostrils, taking in the sights and enjoying the freedom of the infant city of St. Jo. We had half the town at the stables to see the ponies. The offers made for them were without number. One hundred dollars apiece, and even much higher. It would have been a good stroke of business if we had sold and gone back to Detroit and bought more, as they cost only forty dollars a head there, and fifteen to land them in St. Jo.

After getting what information we could respecting routes and river crossings, and making a few purchases, we concluded to pull out, and the next day started up the river on the east side, for Council Bluffs, about one hundred and fifty miles distant. Our reasons for taking this more northern route instead of going directly west, was that there were some settlements on that side of the river, and we could obtain hay and corn of the farmers much cheaper than at St. Jo. We needed it then, as grass had not yet started; besides the distance was not much, if any, greater than crossing the river at St. Jo, and taking the Indian territory, as it was then called.

Our first day's land journey was uneventful, but favorable, and we made about twenty-five miles, pitched our tents on the bottom land near a small creek; fed the ponies; cooked our supper; told stories; talked over our plans for the hundredth time; made our bed and turned in, as happy as so many bugs in a rug. It was my first experience of genuine camping out. I had only before had knowledge of amateur camping out, when a few of us lads would make a night of it in some one of the many great sugar camps around my Ohio home, where we would boil sap, "sugar off," and sleep but little; yet how much of happiness was there, and real fun, for otherwise lonely country boys.

But now we had entered upon the nightly necessities of camping in real earnest, and we were prepared to enjoy it after our day's journey, with the excitements and novelties of our new life, and were soon asleep. We had no premonitory dreams of what we had got to endure before our campings should become a history and a memory. About two o'clock we were awakened by water coming in upon us and into our bed, for we were sleeping on the ground. We hastily got ourselves out of our blankets and found that the whole flat was one sheet of water, and still rising. Dressing as soon as possible, we harnessed the ponies, hitched them to the wagon, and undertook to find high ground. But this was more easily planned than executed. The flat was wide, the night was dark, and just as we were coming to high ground there was a low swale at the foot of the hill with still deeper water, into which the ponies plunged and were soon floundering in bogs and mud. All was dark and in confusion, it rained hard, and all four of us were in the deep and muddy water, trying to loosen and extricate the floundering ponies. We finally got out of the slough with the ponies. Morning came at last, though it seemed long in coming, and showed us a sad and crestfallen party, looking out over a dreary waste of water where we had camped but a few hours before. "This is awful," said one; "I wish I was back home again." However, we soon hitched up again and got our wagon out, which we had been compelled to leave in the slough, and pulled out for a farm-house which we saw about a mile off, and where we got a good warm breakfast and plenty of hot coffee, all for the modest sum of ten cents each. Here we spent the whole forenoon drying our clothes and bedding, when we again set out rejoicing, but with less exalted notions of camping on creek bottoms. We arrived on the fourth day at a little town called Lebanon, consisting of a grocery, a blacksmith shop, a hay-stack and one man, who was proprietor and manager of the whole business. There were about a dozen people there patronizing the grocery and drinking its bad whiskey. Here we met two men, who told us they were camped on the other side of the Missouri, waiting for a few more to join them before starting out. We liked the appearance of the men, who said their party consisted of twenty persons, and our party added would make the proper complement, and urged us to join them. We consented to join them. The ferry-boat, they said, would charge us twenty dollars for crossing with

our wagon and four horses, but that they had a contract
for fifteen dollars, and when they went back they would
tell the boatman that more of their party were coming,
and to be ready to take us over in the morning. Sometimes, they said, it took a whole day to cross, and much
depended on the wind, for if it blew up the river they could
not cross at all, but must wait a calm or reverse wind.
We promised if the wind was favorable to be at the river
the next morning.

In the meantime, we concluded we wanted another horse,
and seeing the men at the grocery had one that suited us,
we asked the price. One hundred dollars was the sum
asked. We offered seventy-five dollars, which they declined. But when they saw we were going to give up the
idea of purchasing at their price, their horse-trading ther-
mometer dropped rapidly several degrees, and until it
stood at seventy dollars, when we closed the bargain.
The horse was a good one, and rather than not have got
him we should have given the sum first named. But I was
not so young and inexperienced in buying and selling horses
in Ohio, as not to know the advantages of a little finesse
in such negotiations. We then bought twenty-five bushels
of corn of the grocery man, and loaded up ready for a
start the next morning. When morning came, the wind
blew down the river, and that settled the point. The wind
was our weather-cock for once. Arriving at the river, we
found everything in readiness for crossing, and the men
from the other side were there to help us over. We crossed
without accident or delay, and went directly up to their
camp, where we met as fine a party of young men as ever

got together. But, poor fellows, little did they know what they had got to encounter or endure within the next three months, and little did they dream that in nine months every one of them would sleep the long sleep that knows no waking.

Our new camp consisted of some abandoned log huts, originally built during the Mexican war, and was called, I think, Old Fort Kearney. There was a dozen or more of them, and our original party took up its quarters in one and stabled our ponies in another. Our new friends had been camping there about a week before our arrival. The following morning being the first of April, we broke camp and pulled out on our long and tedious journey. We were all very heavily loaded, principally with horse feed. Some of the boys had two wagons, one being loaded with corn. We expected to find plenty of green grass before a week's time, but in that we were doomed to disappointment, for the season proved to be much later than usual. There was at first much doubt about our little Canadian ponies standing the journey, with the large American horses, especially such fine ones as the others of our party had, for I think they were the finest lot I ever saw. They had all been selected for the special purpose of crossing the plains. Many had brought them from home and their own farm, where they had been raised and where they had fed and groomed them preparatory to this great journey. They looked upon our ponies as poor little, weak, rural scrubs, in comparison to theirs. We felt a little unhappy that they should depreciate our humble team, but we had to put up with it, only replying that

time would test the comparative merits of the stock. And
surely it did, for in less than a month there was not a horse
in the party but they would have exchanged for the poorest
of our ponies. The American horses had always been
stabled and groomed and had plenty of the best hay and
grain, while ours had lived a rough life, and never knew
stable or grain until we got them. Since then we had taken
the best of care of them and had given them all they could
eat, so they had started on the journey with good heart.
A quart of corn a day to ours was as good as four quarts
to theirs, and when their corn was exhausted we had still
a good supply, although they had twice as much when we
started. On the second day we camped on Salt creek,
where Lincoln, the capital of Nebraska, now stands.

We had hardly been located an hour when the camp was
thrown into a state of excitement by the approach of a
solitary horseman leading two pack mules. He proved to
be the mail post-rider from Santa Fé. He was surprised
on finding we were emigrants, and we were delighted at
meeting the lonely government official. We spent the evening listening to his relation of hair-breadth escapes and
thrilling experiences. He was a good story-teller, but
whether they were all true, or largely imaginary, matters
not now, but we believed them all then. He warned us to
keep a sharp lookout for Indians. The Pawnees, he said,
were friendly and we had nothing to fear from them, which
we found to be true. Our visitor had not been gone more
than two hours, when, having again started, a band of
some fifteen or twenty Indians were seen coming down
upon us. They rode up within about two hundred yards

of us, and all dismounted in front of us and made signs for us to stop. We obeyed the first signal. They then beat their breasts in token of friendship, and advanced towards us. Most of our party had never before seen an Indian, at least a wild one, and it is hardly necessary to remark that they did not wish to see one then. I had in my boyhood been some months among the Sacs and Fox tribe when they were in Iowa, and knew something of their habits, ways and actions; so these were not wholly strange to me. They came up to us, beating their breasts and proffering to shake hands with every one, and seemed very friendly. Some could speak a little English, and probably all of them could speak the Sacs and Fox tongue. I had once learned a few words of the latter language, but it had now nearly faded from my memory. I thought of a word or two and tossed it to their principal spokesman. He caught it and made demonstrations of delight at having met a white man who could speak such classical Indian. Hearing them talk and watching their gestures brought back to memory many more words and signs of meaning, and I soon found I possessed tolerable facilities for social intercourse with the wild man. The Indians for that reason seemed to take a liking to me. I was not a little surprised myself at my success, as I was the youngest of the lot and the boy of the party. I was now inspired with ambition and desired to impress my comrades with my importance as an interpreter of the Indian language, and I lost no opportunity of displaying my linguistic accomplishments. My dozen Indian words were a great vocabulary to my companions. They thought me a professor of the Fox language, and never discovered how superficial their interpreter was. Henceforth I was deemed an important member of our party, and whenever any more Indians came down upon us, I was drafted to go to the front.

This band of Indians traveled with us all day and camped near us at night. The boys did not like this, and I did not quite fancy it, but what could we do? We did not want to offend them, or appear to doubt their friendly disposition towards us. The next morning the chief said to me that there was plenty of deer a few miles ahead, a little off the line of our route, and if I would go with them they would take me to the place. Some thought I had better not go, and I did not myself particularly care about it, but when I saw that they were afraid, that settled the point with me, and go I would and did. We started out ahead of the train and came to a creek where we dismounted and lay down. We had not been there more than half an hour before seven fine deer made their appearance. I seized my gun and was going to draw a bead on one at considerable distance, but they told me to wait and the deer would come nearer to us to drink at the creek, which they did, when I pulled the trigger and a fine buck fell. I felt I was growing taller rapidly. By the time the train came up I had him dressed and we all had a feast of venison. The Indian and the white man for once, at least, dined together, and the interpreter sat at the head of the table. The confidence of my companions was greatly increased in me by the outcome of this last doubtful enterprise, and they congratulated themselves in that they had

INSTINCTS OF THE HORSE.

fallen in with a person who so thoroughly understood the
language and character of the Indian.   At the close of the
banquet we parted in peace and friendship.   The Indian
character had now become somewhat exalted in the esti-
mation of our party; they did not believe it so bad as had
been represented.   But they little knew what was yet to
come.

It may be of interest, as an illustration of the wonderful
instincts of the horse, bordering so closely upon reason and
intelligence in man, that our little Canucks, as they were
now called by all, were very much frightened at the sight
of our late indigenous friends, and would not suffer an
Indian to come near them by night or day, and never
throughout our long journey became any more reconciled
to them than at first—a matter that proved very advantageous to us throughout the journey.   An Indian could
not come within a mile of us but the Canucks would make
it known to us; and if they were out feeding they would
make for camp, and would not be driven out of it.   No
watch dog could have been of better service to us in this
regard.

The rest of the journey to New Ft. Kearney was uneventful save in the occasional killing of a deer or antelope, or
the sight of a straggling buffalo, which would set the boys
wild with excitement, but they deemed it prudent not to
exhaust their horses in chasing them, they not being at
that early season fit to eat; besides the post-rider we had
lately met with had told us that beyond Ft. Kearney
we would see them in droves of hundreds and thousands.
This we thought too tough a story for belief, though we

credited all the rest, and therein we were not unlike the simple and credulous mother, in one of Captain Marryatt's novels, whose boy had been to sea, and whose stories and adventures had become her daily consolation and delight. He told her he had seen in the West Indies rivers of rum and mountains of sugar. This was to her a pleasant surprise, but she had implicit confidence in her truthful son, and only reflected on the happiness of a people so bountifully supplied by nature with the necessaries of life. But when he told her he had seen fish fly, the only truth he had told her, she thought he had been tempted by Satan; that certainly was a fish story. Our company could endorse all other tales of the solitary horseman and post-rider but that of the mighty buffalo herds.

On the morning of the eighth day we reached Fort Kearney. It had just been built, or rather, it was then in process of building. One object of the government was a protection and shelter for emigrants, another a station for dragoons that patrolled the road from Fort Laramie to Santa Fé. We found by this time that our horse-feed was likely to run out, as grass had not yet started, but the commissary could furnish us no provender, but could furnish enough flour for ourselves to carry us to Fort Laramie, on the north fork of the Platte river, about four hundred miles. Our purchase of flour was to the extent of some fifty pounds to a man, and for about three dollars per hundred pounds cheaper than our purchase at St. Jo.

The morning we left the Missouri river, a man started out with a wheelbarrow to cross the plains. He had a bushel of parched corn, his blankets, and nothing else. He

THE WHEELBARROW TRAIN.

wheeled it manfully for several days, but the speed we kept up was too great for him, and he gave out. We took him up and carried him on to Fort Kearney, where the government gave him employment at twenty-five dollars per month. There we left him, and I have never heard of him since. I have several times heard of a man crossing the continent with a wheelbarrow, but I don't believe it was ever accomplished. This man, I am sure, could have performed the feat if any one could. He had all the advantages of youth, strength, courage and will, but I think the enterprise beyond human endurance. There are so many sand dunes, some extending for many miles, so many rivers to cross, besides deep and terrible gorges to traverse, and two ranges of mighty mountains to ascend and descend, that it seems to me impossible. Be it as it may, this man started—and that is all I know of him or his wheelbarrow.

CHAPTER III.

Junction North and South Platte — Snow-Storm — Distress and Suffering—Crossing the South Platte—Ogalalla—Impressions of the Country — North Platte Crossing — Buffalo Herds — Game—Sioux—Trading—Ft. Laramie — Shooting Wagons—Crows —Stealing, a Business Transaction — Pancake Snatching—The Frying-Pan Knock Down.

WE left Fort Kearney the next day after our arrival there, it being the ninth day of April, having made two hundred and eighty miles in eight days. The buffaloes were daily getting more plenty, so much so that we were several times compelled to stop our train to let a herd pass. I really believe I have seen herds five miles long. I won't make it any longer for fear I may be thought trying to go one better on the statement of the Santa Fé post-rider. On the fourteenth, when we were near the junction of the North and South Platte, there came on a snow-storm in the night of about a foot in depth. In the morning the wind rose, strong, fierce and cold—a regular blizzard—which continued for three days. The snow covered the buffalo chips so we could not get them to make a fire, and if we could have got them they were so saturated they would not have burned.

We formed a corral with the wagons by hauling them as

close together as possible, running the pole of the hind wagon under the forward one, and so on, and then huddled the horses inside as close as they could stand. Our corn was getting low and we had to use our flour mixed with corn. We could do without flour ourselves, for we could get plenty of meat of all kinds; so we fed the flour to the horses, without any fear for ourselves. We burnt three wagons to keep from perishing. Never in my experience did I pass three such terrible days, and I hope never to be called to endure the like again. The fourth day came off pleasant, but the snow had drifted so that traveling was almost impossible. As the sun shone bright, we were bound to leave the place where we had suffered so much. The bright sunshine on the snow blinded our eyes and blistered our faces. Some may doubt about our faces being blistered by the snow, but it is a fact, nevertheless. Our progress was very slow through the snow-drifts, and we camped early in the day near an island in the South Platte, where there was an abundance of wood, made a good fire and cooked a warm meal, which we had not had for four days, and felt better. It was getting late in the season, especially for such a storm; but now the sun shone clearly and warm, the snow was fast disappearing, and what was better still, our hopes of green grass soon starting, put us all once more in cheerful spirits. We had some fears about being able to cross the two rivers, South and North Platte, and knowing we were close approaching the first, it was thought best that some of the party should go ahead and select a crossing place. I was one of three selected to go on this service, on account of my supposed influence with all Indian tribes we might meet with, having already had some success with the Pawnees. When we were about twenty-five miles in advance of the train, we fell in with a small band of Pawnees, for we were not yet out of their territory. We were surprised to find that they knew of our coming and were on the lookout for us. They told us the regular crossing was about twenty miles from there, up the river, but that as the river was rising rapidly it would be too high by the time the train would arrive there; so they took us back about six miles and showed us a crossing which they said was better than the one above. They took us across and showed us how we must take advantage of the sand bars. They were friendly, and of great service to us. They warned us to beware of the Sioux, as they were very mean and would lie and steal. We found afterwards that they had told us the truth, in the latter respect certainly, for a bigger set of thieves no one ever fell in with. They told us never to attempt to go straight across a stream, but to strike a current, and follow it up or down until we struck another, and follow it up or down, and so on until we reached the opposite bank. They took us across and showed us how to do it. For this service we gave them sugar, which they were highly pleased with. Their time seemed to be of no object to them, and so they staid with us that night, a thing which we did not much admire, although they had not shown any tendency to steal; yet we had not the most implicit faith in their honesty, and kept a sharp lookout for them The next day the train came up, and we set about crossing the stream. The river was, at this point, we judged, over half a mile wide, but the course of the different currents we had to follow up and down made the journey from side to side nearly two miles. This had to be done with four and six horses, and a man to each wheel. Sometimes all the horses would break through the crust of sand, formed by the pressure of the current running over it, and all would go down as soon as they began to plunge, and our only way was to unhitch, draw them down on to another hard crust in the current below, and all hands man the wagons and drag them out. Sometimes the wagons would be left standing so long the water would wash the crust away from the wheels and down they would go, and we would have to unload and carry everything to a sand bar, then take the wheels off and float the box down, put the vehicle together again, load up, and make another start, only to meet with a similar mishap. The only way was when once started to keep moving as long as possible. Every man of us was in the water from morning till night, and must have traveled in the three days of crossing, ten miles in water up to his waist, for nearly every team required the whole force in its transit. But everything has an end, and so did the crossing of the South Platte river. After a tedious labor of just three days, we camped out in the Ogalalla, about five hundred yards from the river, to avoid musquitoes, which were terribly annoying nights and mornings, which one would hardly believe possible only five days after a severe snow-storm. Nevertheless, it was so. The weather had come off warm, and we had now high hopes of grass, as it had already begun to sprout.

I have often been asked if the country along the Platte

produced grass at that time. I do not think it did so much as now. There was plenty of dry last year's grass when we came along, showing that the year before there had been a good growth. The impression that for a time prevailed that that region of country produced but little or none, resulted from the enormous amount of emigration that followed us, which kept the grass cut down so close that the land was thought to be barren. Almost every one at that time was unfavorably impressed with that region of country, and I thought then, if the government would offer me a patent of all the land we traversed between Fort Kearney and Fort Laramie, I would not accept it; yet hundreds of miles of the same land has since proved to be of the very best quality for both grazing and agriculture. The fact that the region abounded with buffalo at the time we passed, was proof that it was a good range for mighty herds, and the game we killed was very fat; besides. the Indians were there with plenty of horses, all of which looked well for that season of the year. Why should not grass have grown then as well as now (1887), for the country along the North and South Platte is in a high state of cultivation?

The very place where we crossed the South Platte boasts of a town, only three years old, Ogalalla, the county-seat of Keith county, western Nebraska, bordering upon the northeast corner of Colorado. Its population exceeds a thousand. It has two banks, three hotels, three dry goods stores, groceries, furniture houses, a seventy barrel flour mill, and restaurants too numerous to mention. The population of the county is over four thousand, and the country for miles around is equal to any in the east. So one can see that the opinion of many early emigrants was incorrect touching the value of the land.

Ogalalla is the westernmost station but one on the Union Pacific railroad in Nebraska, and here, near the scene of his first sad experience in crossing the continent, after thirty-five years of varied fortunes by land and sea, the narrator has pitched his tent for life among a generous, industrious and enterprising people, where, even but a few short years since, there was but the trail of the buffalo, the Indian and the gold hunter, and calls the goodly town his home.

And now, after this digression, I return to the more serious business of our journey. From the South Platte where we crossed to the North Platte is about seven miles, but we took a western course and did not strike the latter river until we had traveled about fourteen miles, and continued on some distance to a point laid down on the late maps as Ash Hollow, on account of some small ash trees growing in the ravines near the place of crossing. We tried it by sending over some of the men on horseback, who reported favorably. We camped there on the south bank that night and made an early start in the morning, sending over our wagons with boxes or beds all made water tight, and fastened down to the running gear, and two strong cords fore and aft, with four men holding the ropes from the upper side of the stream. This we found answered well, and soon we had two teams crossing over at the same time, and, in the course of the day, had them all on the other side of the river without a single accident, and so the stream which we had most dreaded proved the one that gave us the least trouble.

We were now in high spirits, thinking we were over the worst of it. It is best, perhaps, that nature has ordained the future to be closely veiled from the human mind. True we had met thus far none but friendly Indians—we did not want to. We were like the man who was asked to go out in advance as a scout in search of Indians that had been committing some depredations. "No," said he, "I have lost no Indians, and I don't want to find any." We had not come out into that wilderness in search of the red man, although we kept a sharp lookout for him. Not a night passed but we stationed two men on sentry, relieving them at twelve o'clock and putting on two more till morning. The weather was getting warm, but the grass did not seem to grow. There was, however, an abundance of old grass, which seemed to be much better than on the South Platte. Our corn and flour were nearly exhausted, and we had used none of the latter ourselves. We had hopes of buying some at Laramie, and were bound to make all speed for that place. We were now twenty-three days out and had made over five hundred miles, notwithstanding hindrances by storm and the crossing of two rivers, and had advanced about two hundred miles from where we crossed. At night, around our fires, our experiences were rehearsed and our plans laid for the next day. We had plenty of meat, and if we were out, all one had to do was to go outside the camp a short distance and kill as many antelopes as he wanted; and as for buffalo, they were a troublesome nuisance, often stopping the train till the herd passed. We could shoot into a herd when pass-ing and drop a young heifer or two, dress them, take what we wanted, and leave the rest to spoil—spoil, that was almost impossible. Meat would keep for weeks, even in hot weather. A hard shell would form over the outside and keep the inside fresh and sweet for an incredible length of time.

We were now traveling over thirty miles a day, on an average, towards Laramie. The roads were good, no rivers to cross, and nothing to detain. It was too late in the season to expect any more storms, especially such as we had experienced; the land was rolling and not mountain-ous. We met with but one band of Indians, Sioux, about twenty in number. They rode around us and finally dis-mounted, and one of them exhibited a paper and offered it to us to read. The document had been written by some white man, stating that they were friendly disposed. They wished to traffic with us. We swapped some old under garments, now useless to us but prized by them, for moccasins and trinkets alike useless to us. They were pleased with their good bargain, and rode along with us for a few miles when they left us, beating their breasts in token of friendship. We arrived at Fort Laramie on the twenty-ninth of April, having made a journey of a little over seven hundred miles in twenty-nine days.

This interior fort was built the year before for the pro-tection of emigrants and the convenience of the dragoons that patrol the road between Fort Hall, in Oregon, and Fort Leavenworth, Kansas, as we were told by the officer in command. It was built on a vast plain in the midst of

thousands of acres of cactuses, growing so rank and thick
that it was impossible of approach except by the road.
Thus it was in no danger of being surrounded and surprised by Indians, for they could only gain access by the
road, where a single charge of grape or canister would cut
a wide swath in their ranks. The fort possessed two cannon of ample calibre, on wheels, which were a curiosity to
many interior Indians who visited the fort They looked
into the muzzle and walked around it, treading lightly,
but when it was suddenly and to them unexpectedly discharged, they ran for their lives, and did not return for a
long time, and when they did, they approached cautiously,
and asked if the "shooting-wagons" were loaded. When
told they were, the Indians left, saying, "Shooting-wagons
no good."

The soldiers told us some pretty tough yarns about their
encounters with the Sioux and the Crows—some were true
and others, perhaps, doubtful—but we took them all in.
They had the effect, at least, to make us keep a sharp lookout, to be on our guard, and in that respect they were
harmless, if otherwise we did not receive them in the ut-
most faith. As we were out of flour, the commissary told
us we could have it at cost to the government, including
the freightage, which was sixteen dollars the hundred
pounds. We were willing to pay that price, but were disappointed when he would let us have but fifty pounds per
man. We worked him a little. One party would go and
get two hundred pounds for his party, then the same party
would send another man and get the same amount, but
soon he discovered our scheme and dropped on it, and

would not let us have any more unless all hands in the party came together. We could not ring in on him the second time, but he took it all in good part, however. We remained there and rested our teams for two days. We left there on the second day of May, just about the time we should have left the Missouri river. Before we started, news came in from the Black Hills, brought by the Crows. Little and unimportant news is wonderfully refreshing to those who have been shut up in the interior of the continent for a month, and there is no end to the number of simple questions we all asked the gentlemanly Crows, and I have since wondered they did not get impatient with us; but they seemed to like it, and regarded themselves as of great importance in consequence.

While we were at Laramie, we learned that a few days before our arrival a soldier had stolen the colonel's horse and struck out for California. It was a valuable one, worth about one hundred and seventy-five dollars. We thought strange the colonel did not have him pursued, but he said, "Let him go, it won't be long before he will be back." When we had camped, on the evening of the second day out from Laramie, we saw at some distance a solitary horseman, coming on a little diminutive brute of a horse. We watched him for some time, totally befogged as to who or what he was. He didn't look like an Indian, although he had a buffalo robe around him. The mystery was solved when he rode up and got off—it was a white man. Except the buffalo robe, he was as naked as he was born. He proved to be the soldier that had stolen the colonel's horse. He had rode him, he said, about a hundred miles the first twenty-four hours, and tied up for a few hours to give him a rest, and again started and rode him until the next night, when a band of Crows came down on him and took his provisions, every stitch of his clothing, and his horse, saddle and bridle, gave him the buffalo rug, some jerked buffalo meat and the poorest pony they had, and told him to go back. This with the Crows is not deemed robbing or stealing, but a pure business transaction, not unlike, though in a humbler degree, a modern Wall street operation, though in the latter instance, the winning party rarely contributes even a blanket to cover the nakedness of the party fleeced. The Crows call it swapping. They say the Sioux are mean and will steal—but Crows, "they good Indian, they swap." When they swap, they are pretty sure to get the best of the bargain, especially when they have an opportunity to corner the market, as they did when they dealt with the Laramie soldier.

We fell in with several parties of Sioux, and found they had not been misrepresented touching their pilfering qualities—in fact, they would rob. They would rush and snatch the food we were cooking, and if one would allow them, they were what is called awful bouncers, if they thought one was the least afraid of them. One of them tried his little game on me, but it did not pan out as he had expected. I was cooking some pan-cakes in a frying-pan. He came up to me, saying in a bouncing and swaggering way, "Give me." I shook my head, and said "No." "Yes," said he, and grabbed at those on the tin plate—they fell to the ground. As he stooped to pick them up, I struck him over the head with the hot frying-pan and knocked him sprawling, the grease in the pan flying all over his head and face. He got up and went off, shaking his head in burning pain and muttering terrible anathemas on me, I suppose—certainly they were not prayers or blessings, as I judged from the expression of his countenance. It was all the same to me, however. Whether curses or prayers, I never felt damage or benefit from them. The boys were afraid that my rash act would call down the vengeance of the whole tribe, but instead of that the others seemed to enjoy the joke, for they laughed at him, and he appeared to be ashamed. He did not, however, attempt to help himself to any more pancakes.

CHAPTER IV.

BLACK HILLS—ANTELOPE AND ELK—CANADIAN FUR TRAPPERS—COURT-HOUSE ROCK — CHIMNEY ROCK — HOSTILE CROWS — STRANGE MAN-ŒUVERS—OUR SCOTCHMAN'S SUDDEN SICKNESS—AN INDIAN PRISONER OF WAR — HIS SURRENDER NEGOTIATED — THE PIPE OF PEACE — GEORGE, THE "SQUAW" — TRADING — EMPTY JUG DISCOVERED — WHISKEY LEGAL TENDER—INDEPENDENCE ROCK.

WE were now getting among the Black Hills, a long range of bold mountains, now and then sending down small streams. The hills were of a slippery or soapy nature, and the wagons would slip and slide, particularly if the road was the least sidling. In many places it required the greatest care, and we were compelled to let the wagons down with ropes fastened to the upper side, all hands manning the ropes, and getting them over one at a time, making pretty laborious work. The hills were literally swarming with deer, antelope and elk, the latter the first we had seen. The game did not seem to be afraid, especially the antelope. I went out one morning, not more than four hundred yards from camp, and shot seven, all within fifty yards of the place where I shot the first one. The deer were of the black-tailed kind, and not so large as our eastern deer. There were also some mountain goats, but they were very shy and kept beyond

shooting distance. They seemed to recognize the rule my
father inculcated when I was a child and got in his way,
when he would say, "Stand back, you can see just as
well."

At a place then called La Bont creek, the multitude of
game surpassed all I had ever yet seen. Here we fell in
with a party of Canadian French trappers and fur dealers.
They had four wagons loaded with bales of fur, bound
for St. Jo. A few could speak very indifferent English,
but the larger number only French. They said they had
been from the frontier twelve months, and that for the
last six months had lived solely on jerked buffalo meat
and coffee, never in the time having even seen bread or
flour. Jerked meat is cut in long slips, about a quarter of
an inch thick, and dried over a slow fire, or hung in the
sun four or five days, when it is put away for use. It is
boiled as meat, or used dry in place of bread. It
is very good for a hungry man, and tastes fairly
good, but it will never become popular as a dainty
dish among the epicures of Delmonico's. In 1865,
sixteen years afterwards, I met one of the same party,
Canadian Jo, as we called him, in Australia. He knew
me and told me where he had seen me. I noticed his
English had not much improved in all that length of time.
Coincidences in life are often many and sometimes quite
surprising, and such I deem this one.

We now came to a place called Court-House Rock. The
rock, however, stood about seven miles off our line of
travel, but a conspicuous object. Some of the party got
badly sold in starting on foot to inspect it, thinking it

only about a mile distant, but after walking an hour and finding it still apparently as far off as when they started, gave it up, while others on horseback reached it. It is a high rock in the middle of a great plain, apparently on an artificial mound, the earth gradually sloping from it on every side, and it has the appearance from the road, where we first saw it, of a mammoth court-house, but when approached, they said, it bore no such resemblance. From base to summit it is four hundred feet. Chimney Rock is something over three hundred and fifty feet high, and has the appearance at a distance of an old, dilapidated chimney. I went to see that and climbed to the top. When at the top, and as the sun was about to drop below the horizon, I could see our camp many miles distant in the plain, the men cooking supper, the horses grazing, and what was most strange to my vision, the men looked like toddling children and the horses not more than a foot high; yet all could be seen as plain and distinct as if they had been within two hundred yards, while in fact they were seven or eight miles away, for it took me over two hours rapid walking to reach camp.

The day after visiting Chimney Rock, about ten in the morning, we were surprised by a band of Crow Indians, who came riding down from the northern hills at full speed. There must have been seventy-five or eighty of them. They came within about four hundred yards of us; then suddenly wheeled their horses and rode around us two or three times, at the same time going through many of their warlike motions, drawing their bows as if to send an arrow. Some would ride down furiously close to us, as if they were going straight through us, then suddenly turn and ride back, turning in their saddles and feigning to shoot, and finally return to their party, which had been watching their movements with apparently as much interest as we had been, which was not a little. We expected an attack and closed up our teams as close as possible, but still kept on the move. The men all examined their rifles and pistols. It was my turn to drive that day. We had a Scotchman in our mess, who just then came to me holding his head with both hands. "O, Charlie," said he, "I am so sick." "Are you," said I, "then get up here and drive." I was as glad to get down as he was to get up, as I knew that if the train was attacked the driver would be picked off first. I had not been down five minutes before I saw our train apparently without a driver. I ran around thinking George was really sick and had keeled over, but found he had made a hole among the bags and boxes just big enough to crawl into, leaving his head only just high enough to see the horses. Frightened as I was myself, I could not help but laugh. I knew he was a consummate coward, but I had given him credit for too much pride to let it be known.

The Indians had now been at least half an hour going through their performances, only stopping to let their horses blow, and then start afresh, we still moving on. At last, one more daring than the rest came down on us and went through a like performance, wheeling and pretending to shoot. There was a young fellow in our company named James Pierson, a daring spirit as ever lived, and as good a fellow as he was fearless, who had a splendid riding horse, three-quarters bred, that could run like a deer, for which my pony was no match. But I went to Jim and said, "If that redskin tries that game again, and you will cut him off from the rest, I will ride in and down him." "All right," said Jim. Presently down came the brave again, this time a little nearer. "Come on, Charlie," said Jim, and away we went. I heard our boys calling to us to come back, George's voice above the rest. He had got over the headache. The Indian saw us coming and tried his best to reach his party, but Jim's horse was too fleet for the Indian's pony, and headed him off. He turned only to meet me, with my pistol on him, within a hundred feet. He dropped his bow, pulled in his horse and began beating his breast. With our prisoner between us we rode proudly into camp. When the other Indians saw we had the man, they got off their horses and down upon their knees, beat their breasts and made signs for us to come up to them. We stopped the train and went out to meet them. They professed friendship, pulled out the pipe, got into a line, and asked us to give up our prisoner, which we did. Then we all took a whiff from the pipe, they all the while beating and pounding away on their chests. Jim and myself they complimented with titles, such as "Big Warrior," "Big Man," but when driver Scotch George came to have his pull at the pipe, they said, "Squaw no good," and refused him the pipe, and turning to me said, "coolah (boy), no squaw." So they had noticed George's taking the place of driver and hiding in the wagon. Poor George was rather crest-fallen, for he had been a great brag, always telling what he would do in case of an engagement. He never, so long as I knew him, recovered from the Indian christening of "Squaw"

When the prisoner had been surrendered and the treaty of peace negotiated, trade and commerce succeeded, and traffic began They were ready to swap anything for sugar. They had an American horse—one, I suppose, they had borrowed the year before of the Mormons as they passed along. He was a fine upstanding animal but very poor, and his hair was long and rough. At'first look one would not give five dollars for him. I wanted to buy him but did not know what to give, or what to offer in exchange. They wanted sugar—I offered them money—"no good, they said. Sugar and whiskey were legal tender. I was bound to have the horse, and as I had not used my share of our stock of sugar, and felt rich in the supposed possession of a quart of brandy—my share of the gallon, never having tasted it, I supposed it all in the jug—I was prepared to trade. George earnestly remonstrated against my parting with the brandy; we would want it for sickness, he said. Both the other men were willing, so I agreed to give a pint of sugar and a pint of whiskey. George interposed a final objection—if I treated the Indians, they would follow us and steal the horse back and more with him. But it was of no use, and the boys all said they would stand extra guard for a few nights, and that settled it. I took an empty vinegar bottle, put in about one-third water, got out the gallon jug of brandy, that no one had yet tasted, and filled a pint cup. Judge of our surprise when we found it had been exhausted and watered till it was about the strength and color of pale sherry! But no one was more surprised than Scotch George himself. He charged it upon some of the other boys; but it was of no use, for the cat was out of the bag. His strenuous objection to the trade was the dread of the brandy exposure. He was crestfallen, but did not reform, for when, some days afterwards, a little brandy was needed, the jug was empty. Thus ended the Crow war.

Among the less weightier transactions was the exchange of an old, blue, woolen shirt, that I had worn from the frontier, for a suit of buckskin, shirt and pants, with strips two or three inches in length along the seams. It was a fine and attractive costume when new and the weather was dry, but when the pants got wet in the slums, the legs elongated, and from time to time had to be amputated a few inches—the same with the sleeves of the shirt—but soon, however, when the weather became dry and warm, the legs of the pants withdrew to a point above my knees, and the sleeves of the shirt could not be coaxed down below my elbows. I never afterwards aspired to Indian fashions or patronized the redskin tailor.

We next came to Independence Rock, so named, it was said by some, by Colonel Fremont, who stopped there one Fourth of July—by others who say because it stands out on the plain, away from any other eminence. It is one solid, grand bowlder, probably the largest in the world, covering, at least, ten acres of ground, and is between two hundred and three hundred feet high. Whatever the origin of its name, the rock is there, with many thousand names of visitors inscribed thereon, some with chisel and others with paint. I undertook to chisel my name there, but soon became discouraged and gave it up. We remained a day and rested our horses, which had begun to fag, and were falling away and getting weak for the want of green grass.

Resting upon the ground on the sunny side of the mighty bowlder, a boy of seventeen, unlettered and unread, to whom geology was a term almost unknown, and the theory of the Ice Age not yet developed, instinct alone prompted the mind to contemplation—to questions unanswerable—as the one invariably propounded by the child when told by his mother who made him—"Who made God?" Whence came this loose, separate, independent bowlder rock—mightiest of the mightiest—in the centre of this vast green and grassy plain, on the roof of the continent, miles away from all other

> "Crags, knolls and mounds, confus'dly hurled,
> The fragments of an earlier world?"

As the finite cannot comprehend the infinite, so I was left to ponder upon the incomprehensible mystery, even unto this day, of the genesis and history of Independence Rock.

The Sweet Water river is close by the rock. It is about one hundred and fifty feet wide, and we crossed it on snow that had slid down in an avalanche, completely burying it. The snow was frozen on the top, forming a crust capable of bearing our horses and wagons. A short distance from where we crossed, there was a crack in the snow that enabled us to see the river running beneath. We let down a rope to the water, which on measuring we found to be twenty-four feet from the surface of the snow. It was a perfectly safe bridge for miles. The stream forces itself through a split mountain. The rift is not more than two hundred yards wide, and the rocky walls rise over three hundred feet above the water. It is a fearfully grand sight to look down into the chasm where the water rushes, dashing against the bowlders and forming foam and spray almost equal to Niagara Falls. It is called Devil's Gate. I do not wish to pass an opinion upon the appropriateness of the name, but I feel pretty sure that if one entered the gate, he would soon be launched into the presence of his Satanic majesty or landed in the realms of bliss.

CHAPTER V.

WE were now approaching what was called the South Pass, or the summit of the Rock mountains, where the waters divide—one making for the Pacific, the other the Atlantic. We were within twenty miles of the summit, and many were our speculations concerning its topographical appearance. Some thought it would be a great mountain to ascend and descend, but all were agreeably disappointed when we found it was a gradual and hardly perceptible ascent to a point where, for the first time, we saw the water running in a westerly course. We thought concerning the summit something as did the Irishman on board ship about to cross the equatorial line, for which he had kept a sharp lookout but did not see, and who, when asked about his experience when crossing the line, said, "Devil dam of a line did I see."

The country now for about eighteen miles on was as level as a house floor and about twenty miles wide from hills to hills, when we came to a fork in the roads, or rather trails, to a place called Subblet's Cut-off, one leading northwest, towards Oregon, the other a little south of west, which went directly to Salt Lake City and the Mormons. After much consideration and discussion it was put to vote, and the latter route carried, although it was a diversion of some two hundred miles from the direct route. The object was to rest and replenish our stock of provisions. After passing the summit the grass gradually improved, and being mixed with the old did not hurt, but greatly strengthened our poor and weakened horses, for they got about equal amounts of each. We were in good spirits, feeling that we were on the last half of our journey, and began to think our greatest troubles over. There was a general rejoicing in camp that night—story telling and song singing. Conviviality is a wonderful cure for past afflictions.

Our next place of note was the crossing of Green river— that wonderful central continental stream which has its source near Yellowstone National Park and the fountain-head of the Missouri, and empties into the Colorado as the Missouri does into the Mississippi. When we drove down to the river we were surprised to find a band of at least two hundred Shoshone Indians camped on the western bank. It was late in the afternoon, and it would take till dark to cross, and then we would be compelled to camp among this strange tribe, an idea that was not pleasant to contemplate, and so we concluded to camp where we were, and commenced to turn out our horses. We had hardly let them loose when some of the tribe came over to

us and gave us to understand that we must cross that
night, for in the morning, they said, the river would be too
high to cross. At first we thought it a scheme of theirs to
get us among them and rob us in the night. Upon further
consideration, we thought if their purpose was to rob us
the river was no hindrance to them, and so we concluded
to cross. The whole band turned to and lent a hand in
crossing. "Many hands make light work," and so it was in
this instance, at least it made quick work. The Indians
worked manfully, and I don't think we were over two
hours in crossing the now famous river. They all seemed
to be very friendly, and the only matter they bothered us
about was their extreme anxiety to trade. For the most
worthless article we had they were ready to swap something equally valueless to us. We satisfied them pretty
well for their services, which had been valuable to us. In
the morning we found, as they had told us, the river
swollen bank to bank, and which would have caused us
great trouble and loss of time had we not taken their
advice.

They took every means to amuse us, even to the getting
up of a horse race, and inviting us to enter our ponies and
blooded stock, and compete with them for the royal redskin "cup." We explained to them that our horses were
all handicapped by hard service and sharp bones, and
could not compete at the Indian "Derby" with the racers
of the Shoshone nation, on the banks of Green river. They
intimated that we were altogether too modest in our
claims by pointing out, as a worthy horse to enter, Jim
Pierson's "Dexter"—the same with which he had clipped

the wings of the Crow. They are, generally speaking, good judges of a horse.

The next morning, when we started, they struck their tents and traveled all day with us, and there were many amusing scenes in the cavalcade. Ponies packed so one could see only a big bundle of traps moving; another pony carried a big basket on each side with three or four little Indians in each; still another wee bit of a pony would stagger under the weight of two, and sometimes three, robust and heavy buck Indians. The men all rode while the squaws were all on foot, and most of them staggering under a heavy load. Chivalry seemed to have been but partially developed among the Indian tribes, for while the man went in quest of adventure, and revelled in jousts and bouts, they seemed to have no lady-love to protect, or whose smiles of approbation they considered worthy to win. The Indian woman is a beast of burden and a slave. Civilized man is more kindly and generous towards woman. He lets her do as she pleases—perhaps he can't help himself—pays her dry goods bills, or fails; lets her have her own separate property, and his own too, when he wants to keep it from his creditors; indulges her in occasional hours of relaxation by holding the baby. In fact, he debars her of no rights which he himself enjoys, saving the right to vote and to "speak in meeting"— which last even Paul would not allow.

They camped with us the second night, and in the morning left us, manifesting the strongest tokens of friendship. Since we had passed the summit our road had been changeable, with many small mountain streams to cross, one of which was so serpentine that we crossed it twenty-seven times. The snow was rapidly melting, and every little stream was swollen to full banks. There was a place in our route called Steamboat Spring Valley, which was interesting to travelers from the circumstance of its containing certain very active hot springs, whose intermittent puffs of steam could be seen at a great distance, and which seemed wonderfully like an approaching steamboat. Upon arriving at the place several springs were found puffing away—all more or less hot—one, in particular, certainly near the boiling point, which was said to be unfathomable, which would bubble and boil at the surface for a minute or so, and then belch forth to the height of two or three feet and then subside for two or three minutes, and then repeat the process. It was, at least, a vivid reminder of the story of the Dutchman and his son, who, in crossing the country, had camped near a hot spring; but all innocent of such a wonderful phenomenon, he started out to get a refreshing drink while his son was unyoking the oxen. He got down on his knees, but took in, instead of cold, a mouthful of hot water. Ejecting it quicker than he had sipped it, he told Hanse to yoke up the oxen quick—saying, "Hell is not one mile from this place, sure." Often within a few rods, or even feet, of one of these hot springs, there will be a spring of ice cold water.

Game was getting scarcer very fast after crossing the summit, only a few antelope and deer, no mountain goats, no elk, nor jack rabbits, which, perhaps, I have not before mentioned, but which bear a strong resemblance to the En-

glish hare. There is also the sage hen, something like the
partridge or the New Zealand hen. They are a fine-looking
bird, but when cooked they are not eatable, being so
strongly tainted with the wild sage bush, which is their
sole subsistence. The wild sage is mostly found on barren
land, and the Laramie country produced the most exten-
sive fields of it. As for the Indians, I found the Pawnees
the best tribe, the Shoshones the next, but to take their
word each tribe was good, but their neighbors were
represented as all liars and thieves. The Sioux had that
name among emigrants. All tribes I ever talked with
said the Crows would rob, or "swap," as they called it.
But of all the tribes that we had met with thus far, the
Shoshonees alone did not steal from us. Nevertheless, all
Indians are at least notorious vagabonds and beggars.

While the days were warm, the nights were now very
cold, and we suffered much, for we were wet during the
day in crossing streams and lay in wet blankets nights,
not one of us having a stitch of dry bedding. We were,
however, happy in one thing, and that was that food was
good and our horses were improving every day. I never
before saw grass that horses would fatten on in so short
a time, and do so much work as they will on this western
prairie grass; nor did I ever see old last year's grass that
had the substance in it like this in and around the Rocky
mountains. The reason is, there is not so much rain and
it cures before frost comes; the substance and sweetness is
dried into it instead of being dried out of it.

Now we have come to Ft. Bridger, which now, after
thirty-eight years, is known upon the map as being in the

southwest corner of Wyoming, close to the border of Utah. It was named after the man who built it twenty-seven years before, and still lived in it. It was dark before the train reached there, and three of us rode ahead, but it being further than we thought for, the gates of the Bridger fortress were closed for the night. We knocked for admittance. He asked who was there. "A party from the frontier," we responded. "When?" he asked. "This spring," we replied. "Impossible!" said he. But we proved our case to his entire satisfaction by showing him the St. Louis papers. He took us in and treated us very hospitably. He had a squaw and two children, a boy and girl, half casts, of whom he seemed to be very fond. They were about fourteen and sixteen, respectively. Old Jim, as the lord of the castle was called, was anxious for us to hear them read, which we did. Madam Bridger, the squaw, cooked us a good supper, making some light biscuit. I don't know but that it was because we were very hungry, but certainly I thought they were the best I had ever eaten. At all events, they were the very best I had ever eaten of a squaw's baking. We had a good dry bed of buffalo rugs—the first dry bed for many a night—and I need not say that though a lad of only seventeen, worn out and tired as I was, I did not require rocking to induce sleep after getting into a warm bed.

The train came in about noon the next day and camped. Bridger, or Old Jim, gave us a remarkable history of himself. He said that the name by which he was known was an assumed one, that he was a native of Virginia. He said that when a boy of sixteen he fell into disgrace, and in consequence thereof ran away, and that his family had never known of his whereabouts as he knew of, as he had changed his name and had never written home. Joining a band of trappers he came out there, where he had remained ever since. He claimed to be very rich, having made his money in the fur trade, and after the Mormons commenced to come to Salt Lake he made much money out of them by trading in horses, taking their worn out ones and getting the full value of his in money as "boot." According to his own story, he was an unscrupulous sharper with very strong tendencies towards rascality.

We started next day for Salt Lake City, a distance of one hundred and twenty miles. We were in hopes to reach there in five days, but we were disappointed. The first stream to cross was Black river—not much of a stream, but we had to take our wagons to pieces and ferry across in wagon boxes, a tedious operation, as the ground was boggy leading to the approaches, consequently all our luggage, and even the wagons had to be carried to the river from the foot of the spurs—in some instances a hundred yards. A rope had to be run across the stream, by some one swimming across and carrying a cord in his teeth attached to a rope, and pulling it over. After this was made fast, a wagon box, well corked and pitched so as to be water tight, was launched, and the work of ferrying commenced. It was a tedious and laborious job. Then Black Fork river had to be crossed. The first time it was accomplished without difficulty, but the second time we had to swim our horses. It was difficult to make our horses take the stream. We had to push them in, but their instincts protested, and they would turn and come back.   My little horse Billey was the best leader of all, and was always selected for that service, especially where the current was swift.   I had implicit confidence in him, and had become careless.   I jumped onto him without taking off his harness.   I pulled off my pants and took them on my arm.   We had reached the middle of the stream when Billey caught his hind foot in one of the traces and suddenly rolled over on his side and floated down stream, while I became confused, not thinking to cut the harness and let him free.   I jumped from him and went ashore, but seeing my little horse still struggling in the middle of the stream, my presence of mind returned, and, taking my knife in my teeth, I started back for poor Billey, cut the harness and freed him, and soon had him on shore. The current was strong, the water cold, and we must have been in the water half an hour.   I became chilled, had the cramps in coming ashore, thought every stroke would be the last, and it would had not good Jim Pierson seen my difficulty and stripped and come to my rescue.   I was brought ashore and laid out on the ground perfectly benumbed.   They rubbed me and ran for the brandy, but it had all evaporated through old George, and nothing was available but some of the cayenne pepper.   They rubbed me with that and gave me some internally, which brought me around.   In less than three hours I was swimming the stream for the third time with a cord in my teeth, but my horse was never good in the water after that.

Webber river next gave us considerable trouble, a crooked river which we had to cross several times, of swift current, where the wagons had to be held by ropes.   On this river is the famous Echo cañon. At some places in the cañon, which is some miles in length, one may talk in a common tone of voice, and he will get no less than three distinct repeatals of the words he has spoken. Some days the echo is much more distinct than others. The scenery in some places is unspeakably grand. The cañon is about two hundred yards wide, with perpendicular walls four hundred feet high. At some points, one may see the mountain goats skipping from rock to rock, where one would hardly think a fly could hang on. They are very shy, and it is almost impossible to get near enough to shoot one. We occasionally had an opportunity to inspect the carcass of one who had departed this life, leaving his head and horns, which we found to be about as much as we could carry. We had now got past the region of game—only now and then an antelope—buffalo from herds of thousands had dwindled down to two or three at the most, a few ducks, and that was all. Saw some signs of the grizzly bear as soon as we had passed the summit and began to descend the western slope, but the terrible beast himself we had not seen. He was doubtless at home, but none of us were ambitious of making his acquaintance, so passed his door without leaving our card or knocking.

We now left Echo cañon and passed over to another, and up it for fifteen miles, leading over the divide, or low mountain range which separates the Green River valley from the Salt Lake basin. Of all the trials we had met with in our long journey, this was the chief. The gorge was filled with snow from bottom to top and was melting, and streams of water from the sides were rushing in.

The horses would break through the softening crust and have to be dragged out; the wagons had to be taken to pieces and carried; and, worse still, when night came we had to take the horses back to Webber cañon to feed. This Herculean labor lasted five days, when finally we reached the summit to find our ample reward in the most beautiful prospect on this earth. Seventeen miles away down the gentle western slope lay the beautiful, but then little, village of Salt Lake, as plain to the naked eye as if only half a mile away. Beyond the village, Salt Lake, eighty miles long, glistened in the sun, its remotest shore as distinctly visible as the village itself. Away to the south, as far as the eye could reach, was one broad, beautiful, level plain, covered already with a carpet of deepest green. All this loveliness of lake and landscape was bordered and framed by snow-capped mountains whose silver summits seemed to touch the blue vault of heaven. Such were my impressions of Salt Lake City and valley then, and never since, in all my travels, has that picture faded from my memory or been surpassed by any other.

Not one of our company but enjoyed these beauties of nature. We celebrated the day by pitching our camp on the summit and dining on the best our larder afforded. It was our last meal on the first half of our journey. At three o'clock we arrived on the ground, about two miles out of the city, where, I am told, the new fort now is, though I have not been there since. Here, on the nineteenth day of May, 1850, we camped for a few days, it being our forty-ninth day out, and having traveled thirteen hundred miles from St. Louis.

CHAPTER VI.

SALT LAKE CITY—HOSPITALITY—MORMON WOMEN—ANXIETY FOR NEWS
—NEEDLES AND THREAD—BRIGHAM YOUNG—SUNDAY AT THE TEMPLE
—A RACE WITH A SHOWER—LAUGHING LADIES—DISTANCE DECEP-
TIVE — COMFORTING ASSURANCES — INDIANS ALL BAPTIZED—OGDEN
PARK—SUDDEN DEATH—BEAR RIVER—THE VALLEY—THEN AND
NOW.

NEVER were people more surprised than were those
at Salt Lake City at such an early arrival. It was
unprecedented, impossible; they would not believe we had
come all the way from the Mississippi until we showed
them St. Louis papers. The hospitality of the people of
Salt Lake City was unbounded. No strangers were ever
before or since taken in and treated more kindly by any people on this earth than we were by them. Women in particular were as kind as mothers and sisters to sons and
brothers returned after long absence. They would stop
us on the streets, and call to us from the doors of their
houses to come in, so anxious were they to learn where
we came from, hoping to hear through us from their old
home in the states, or possibly from England, Sweden,
Denmark, and even from the borders of Finland. They
invariably asked us to eat, and would hardly take no for
an answer.

We remained in Salt Lake three days, going among the people, trading any little articles we had for flour, which, by the way, was a scarce article even with them, as all their flour was ground in hand mills and sifted. We bought it by the pint measure, paying thirty cents a pint. Where we traded for sugar we got two pints for one. A spool of thread would buy almost anything of the women, and, as most of the boys' mothers had fitted them out bountifully with needles and thread, they were thus enabled to drive a brisk trade with the Mormon ladies, especially in the line of vegetables, that being the first season of plenty with them. Brigham Young, priest, prophet and king of the Mormon faith, was then in the full vigor of life. He visited our camp and conversed with us on our journey, but neither interfered with us nor had anything to offer offensive or unpleasant. Some of our men attended services at the temple on Sunday, and were treated with the same civility they would have a right to expect from any other class of worshipers. I shall ever feel kindly towards the Mormon people. I never speak evil of the bridge that has carried me safely over the stream. Salt Lake, in my time, was only in its infancy. The Mormons had only sent on a party in 1847 to find a place for settlement, and in 1848 was the first emigration, and it is wonderful how much they had accomplished in two years. They had already many farms under considerable improvement; and as for the future city, it was handsomely laid out in squares, with irrigating streams running through the principal streets, combining in this respect, in a happy degree, the elements of novelty, utility and comfort. About a mile and a half out of town were springs of hot, warm and ice-cold water. They were utilized for bathing purposes. The men monopolized the establishment four days in the week, the women two.

While riding out on a trading expedition for flour and vegetables, I suddenly looked around and discovered a heavy shower of rain which seemed to be close on me. I expected to be drenched to the skin in a moment. Spying a house about half a mile distant, I put my horse to the run, never once looking over my shoulder, but every moment expecting a bath. I could hear it pouring in torrents back on the mountain side, and I spurred the pony on at his full speed. At last I arrived at the house, there to meet five women laughing hard enough to burst steel corsets, had they worn them. I inquired the cause of their laughter, and judge of my surprise when they said they were laughing at me. "It never rains in this valley," they said. I looked back, and there, surely, was the rain pouring down not half a mile off, as it seemed to me. "Well," said I, rather indignantly, "you will see rain here, in this God selected country of yours, in less than three minutes." I could not believe them when they told me that that shower was over five miles away, on the mountain side. "But," said I, "it is not over half that distance to the top of the mountain." They said it was over twenty miles. However, I was soon on friendly terms with these laughing women and effected a pretty good trade with them, and rode away, they telling me in happy humor that if I saw another shower of rain not to break my horse's neck trying to run away from it, if I did not like to be laughed at

A RACE WITH A SHOWER.

in Salt Lake valley. When I returned to camp, one of the boys related a similar experience. I laughed at him, but took good care to keep my own adventure to myself.

On leaving our Mormon friends, they all comforted us with the assurance that we need have no fear of the Indians, the Piutes, as they had all joined the congregation of the Latter Day Saints, the chief only a few days before having been baptized. We felt glad to know that the noble chief and his whole tribe had secured through tickets and a front seat in the happy hunting grounds of the hereafter; but somehow our faith was not implicit that when we met him he would give us a "free pass" on our temporal journey. Ogden Fork, as it was then called, thirty-eight miles due north from Salt Lake City, was our next objective point, where Ogden City now stands, on the Webber river, at the junction of the Union and Central Pacific railroads. The afternoon after leaving Salt Lake City, I was walking with one of our boys, both of us building castles in the air, when he told me his sole ambition was to get money enough in California to return and buy a farm and make a home for his widowed mother and a sister, younger than himself, that he had left behind. His father, he said, had died when he was but ten years old, leaving his mother in humble circumstances; but she had struggled through and managed to give him a good education, and now he only wanted to make enough to place her in comfort in her old age. I left him leading a pack horse and walking. Ten minutes later the pack turned, frightening the horse, which sprang forward, striking him between the shoulders with his fore feet, and knocking him down and his breath out of his body. We carried him under the shade of a tree near by. Not knowing what else to do, and remembering what my brother, the doctor, had told me to do in case of an accident of the kind, I bled him. He seemed to revive for a short time, but gradually sank back, and died in about three hours. We buried him under the tree where we first carried him and where he died. Poor fellow! It was a sudden termination of his young life and all his fond hopes. I have often thought of his poor mother and sister of whom he had spoken so recently, with his eyes glistening with tears of affection. Unfortunately, the poor fellow was a stranger to us all. We had met him only upon the start, and none knew his name or the address of his poor mother. The labors and anxieties of such a journey are so exhausting to the body and absorbing to the mind that we rarely get even the name of an associate, much less a knowledge of his history and family. So it was in this case. I have often wondered if she ever heard of his sad end. Parties like ours do not communicate so freely as they ought to. I have known persons intimately for years, and after all only knew them as Tom or Charley, without inquiring further. We don't like to appear inquisitive. I once knew a man in California by the name of H. G. Nichols, for something over two years, and we were almost as intimate as brothers. One day we were talking, and both suddenly found that we were born within three miles of each other, he in the town of Twinsburg, Ohio, and I in Aurora, and both knew each other's family. On another occasion I was speaking of a young lady and an incident that occurred at a dancing party when she, after dancing, walked out onto the balcony of the hotel and fell to the sidewalk. A party I had known for years began to cross-question me about the incident, and facetiously asked me if I was there. Thinking he disbelieved me I was annoyed, and I said, "No, but perhaps you were." "Yes," said he, "I was." "Now tell me who you are," said he. "I had always supposed you from Kentucky." "And," said I, "I always supposed you were from Missouri"—and that is what we called him. He proved to be Morris Meeker, and when, recently, I returned to Ohio, I went by his request and the promise I made him, and saw his father and sisters in Cleveland. I only speak of this to illustrate how long persons may be acquainted and yet know nothing of their family or history. If persons so situated as we were would only be more communicative, more fathers and mothers would learn the fate of their sons, if death or calamity overtook them far from home.

At a nameless stream, a few miles north of Ogden Fork, which empties into an arm or bay of Salt Lake, we encountered the first serious embarrassment of the second half of our journey. We were two days in crossing this comparatively unimportant stream. Its approach was a quagmire for two hundred yards. It was flooded from bank to bank with the melted snow of the eastern range of mountains, and the current was the swiftest we had yet seen. But it had to be crossed, and we went at it, taking our wagons to pieces and carrying them, piece by piece, across the swampy ground. One of the party, whom we called "Sorrel," a red-haired man, whose name I also

never knew, swam the stream with the fish line in his
teeth, while one man in a tree paid it out to him. This
was to keep the line out of the swift current of the stream
as much as possible, that the swimmer might not be handicapped. Time and perseverance accomplish all things.
One boat was launched, but the current was so strong we
could take but small loads, but we could get them across
as fast as they could be brought to us across the swamp.
It took the whole day and until ten o'clock at night to
accomplish this part of the job. The next day we went
about getting the horses over. They could not cross the
swamp, so we had to go up the stream about four miles
before we could find a place where we could get the horses
in, and the higher up the swifter the current. We had men
on both sides looking for a place, for it required not only
to get in, but to get out as well. The horses seemed to
know the danger as well, if not better, than ourselves, for
it was almost impossible to get them near the stream.
When once you could get one into the stream, the others
would generally follow.

I was called on to lead the way, or ride the leading
horse. The best swimmer was brought to the front, for
poor Billey was wholly demoralized after his struggle in
Black Fork. The horses were now all brought to the
bank. I mounted the leader and he was then pushed
bodily into the stream, and the others followed. No
sooner had we struck the water than the current drew us
under, the horse floundering and I hanging to his neck,
only my two hands sticking out, and going down stream
at the rate of at least eight miles an hour, and all the

other horses in the same manner, none having any more power over the current than if they had been shot from a cannon. We were taken down in this manner for over a mile, when the horse I was riding, or rather hanging to, struck the opposite shore. No sooner had he struck than I was on my feet on the bank, holding him by the bridle and singing out at the top of my lungs for help. One can judge of the rate of speed we floated when the boys on either bank could not keep up, running at the top of their speed. The other horses were swept down past me like shot; but as fortune or Providence would have it, there was a bend in the river about three hundred yards below, and there the other horses landed. It was a sloping bank, and they all walked out. The boys soon came down to me and lifted my horse bodily out of the water. We were now all on the right side of the river without losing a horse or meeting with any other serious accident, and putting our wagons together we went on our way rejoicing.

We had now fair sailing on to Bear river, which is the largest river emptying into Salt Lake from the north. We struck it at a point in the valley about eighty miles from Salt Lake City. It had given us a great deal of anxiety, as they told us in the city that we might as well stay there as to go up and wait there for the new party at Salt Lake City to come, which we tried to persuade to come with us, as they had three fine boats ready to put into the stream; but they declined, saying it was too early, that they were not going up there to wait a month for emigration, so we went without them. Upon reaching the river we were agreeably surprised. Although it was a wide stream and much swollen, the current was slow, and all we had to do was to man our wagon-bed ferry-boat, and two men with spades paddled across, a third man standing at the hind and paying out the rope. Within half an hour from our arrival on its bank we were busy running our wagons and traps over, and within five or six hours we were, horses and all, safe on the western shore. Thus we were detained only a little over half a day at the stream, the crossing of which we had dreaded as much, if not more, than all others on our journey.

We were now in the extreme north of Salt Lake valley. At that time it was perfectly wild; there was no settlement, not even so far north as Ogden. The country was one beautiful, level plain—the bottom of a once great inland sea of which the present salt sea is but a miniature survival. The plain was dotted with thin patches of timber, especially near the numerous small streams that trickled down from the snowy mountains. Now this lovely valley is thickly settled with a teeming and industrious population—a great producing agricultural country, dotted with pleasant farm-houses and thriving and growing villages, with homes of comfort and even luxury, where the most delicious fruit grows almost spontaneously.

CHAPTER VII.

Fort Hall—Soda Springs—Another Party—Disagreement—Humbolt River—The Sink—The Lake—The Desert—Suffering—
Alkali Water—Digger Indians — Surprised — The Killed—A
Death Avenged—Our Loss—Starvation—Boiled Badger—Ex-
haustion—Mental Weakness—Childish Petulance.

LEAVING Bear river, our route bore northwest up a
gradual rise for about one hundred and fifty miles
until we reached Subblet's Cut-off, which I before mentioned as the route where we made a diversion from
the most direct line to go down to Salt Lake. Had
we pursued the direct course, then we would have
been some two hundred and fifty miles farther on our
journey. Here was Fort Hall, and also some soda springs.
The water when first taken out had all the effervescence
and sparkling qualities of the domestic or manufactured
article. When we reached the forks, we were surprised to
find a piece of board put up, on which was written in
bantering style an invitation to "come on." As we had
been leading all others thus far in the journey, it was
now a little humiliating to find a party two days ahead
of us. We resolved, however, to overtake them. For

three days we made at least fifty miles a day, and on the third day we came up with them, and we camped together that night, and for about a week traveled together. The party we called the Ohio party, some being from Pickaway county and others from Canton, Stark county. There was a spirit of rivalry between the two parties to see which could outdo the other in progress. Finally the weaker teams began to give out and fall behind. Some were rather inclined to be vexed at those who were unnecessarily hurrying onward. Not long, however, before there was loud murmur and complaint, secession and a split. Some of our own party falling behind, together with some of the Ohio party, as we called the new party, and being about equally divided, we bade good-by to the balance of the original company we had thus overtaken, and pursued our journey without further entangling alliances with foreign nations or companies.

We were now traveling down Humbolt river, named in honor of the famous German traveler, having struck it near its source, at a point where now is Elko, a station of the Central Pacific railroad. We followed it down three hundred miles, tributaries constantly coming in until at last it becomes a pretty respectable river. After two hundred and fifty miles it gradually diminishes, and at the end of fifty miles more it sinks into the earth and entirely disappears, unless possibly to rise as a spring in the bottom of Humbolt lake. It is a reminder of the legendary story of the river in China where Cublai Khan built, in the thirteenth century, a summer palace on the Alph, near where it is said to sink into the earth and is thenceforth

forever lost, and to which Coleridge alludes in his weird
poem, the opening stanza of which runs thus:

> " In Xanadu did Cublai Khan
> A stately palace dome decree,
> Where Alph, the sacred river, ran
> By caverns measureless to man,
> Down to a sunless sea."

This is the famous sink of the Humbolt. Any one who
went to California by this overland route in the early
days, and conversed with another of like experience, was
sure to hear again and again of the Humbolt, the sink, and
the desert. Upon our arrival at the sink, about ten o'clock
in the morning, we camped, intending to give our horses
rest for the day, and cross the desert by night. Here soon
a division of opinion developed itself among the party as
to which of the routes should be taken. Some were for
taking the hilly and more northerly route bearing towards
Oregon; others, and the majority, were in favor of the
more southerly route, more directly towards California,
but involving the desert country. I protested with spirit
against the desert route. About three o'clock in the afternoon I struck out alone on a tour of reconnoitering and went
down the southerly route five or six miles, where the road
still bore directly south as far as I could see. I turned
back fully believing that I had seen enough to convince
the others that I was right and they were wrong, but when
arriving in camp and reporting, I found them unchangeable
in behalf of the desert route. I persuaded one of them to
go with me to the top of a hill on the northern route to
take observation of the country. This settled it with me,

and I was in hopes our report would influence the majority, but those who had the most to say seemed to have the least knowledge of the geography of the country. They had desert on the brain, and desert they were bound to have. I remonstrated again, showed them how it was laid on the map. It did no good, for instead of influencing them, it seemed to touch their pride, or rather vanity. The idea of a seventeen year old boy attempting to dictate to, or even instruct grown up men, was preposterous! But they soon wished they had followed the boy's advice. By not doing so the majority lost their lives.

At half past eight o'clock of a June evening, we started on that ill-fated route, with all the water our vessels would hold, some even carrying a bucket in their hand. They expected to cross the desert by daylight the next morning. Daylight came, but it brought the most dismal and dreary prospect men ever beheld. O, our poor famishing horses, to say nothing of ourselves! I then tried to have them return to the Humbolt sink—but no, this was the true route. Then, with those who were so wise we traveled on till ten o'clock, when we came to one of those sand mounds, or dunes, on the north side of which were two small lakes, and some coarse, rough bunches of grass, which, when we first saw them, raised our hopes, and even I began to hope that, after all, I was wrong in my conjectures, and that my companions were right. Now one of our party, a wiseacre, such as Artemus Ward would call a "knowledgeous cuss," commenced to ridicule me upon my knowledge, or assumed knowledge of the country, saying "they would have looked well to have followed the advice of a kid that had just left his mother—that it was a pity she had not spanked me before I left home and taken out some of my self-conceit." I told him the right of such discipline I still acknowledged as the prerogative of my mother, but of no other human being; and if he thought he could do the duties of such office, he was then and there welcome to try the experiment. Though ill-tempered and insulting, he did not then proceed to violence.

When we arrived at the lakes, judge of our surprise and disappointment on finding the water of the strongest alkali. Some of the horses got a few swallows before they tasted it; others we succeeded in keeping away. We found some springs near by, but they were hot, some boiling. Resting our horses here for an hour, we again started, and pushed on over the dreary waste of sand till night. The day, fortunately, had been cool and cloudy. Our prospects, however, were as gloomy as ever; but the horses must have rest, to say nothing of ourselves, who were in anything but a sweet temper, everybody blaming his neighbor, and every one coming in for his share of the blame except me. As I had fought so hard against the route from the start, no one presumed to blame me, not even the smart aleck who had ridiculed the kid.

Old Tiger, the horse we bought before crossing the Missouri, got so much of the alkali water that he was getting weaker every hour. All, in fact, were failing except the Canadian ponies; they were all right and plodded right along as though nothing had happened. We laid over until midnight and then started for—God only knew where, for we all confessed we did not. We made but

SORROW OF THE DESERT.

poor headway that night, and when morning came we were on the same shingle lava that rung like a bell when the horses stepped on it. There was some change in the prospects in the morning. We could see some low shrubs ahead, and some signs of vegetation, little patches of sword grass with sorry attempts at better grass growing. Presently the mules began to bray, and the Canucks to prick up their ears, sniff, and push ahead. We knew we were coming to water. O, how impatient was both man and beast to reach the expectant water! Words are value-less, and fall dead and meaningless in the attempt to decribe such a scene to one who has not had a similar experience. Poor old Tiger, who had been staggering along, soon stumbled and fell. We pulled off his pack and let him lie. Some were for killing him, but Costler and myself would not permit it. From that time on the horses began to drop, one after another, until five succumbed to the terrible effects of famishing. We left them as we left Tiger, and went on. As all misery must have an end, so did ours, when at last we reached a little creek of fresh water and plenty of grass. But now came the tug of war; our horses and mules rushed with fury for the water, and it was almost impossible to control them. Mules were braying, horses pawing and men swearing, a wild and crazy orchestra in the desert. As soon as we got the sur-vivors watered and turned out to grass, some of us started back with water for the poor beasts that had fallen by the way. The farthest, old Tiger, was about five miles back. What was our surprise when we met the old fellow, staggering on a few rods and then stopping to rest. We gave him about a gallon of water. He stood for a while begging hard for more, like Dickens' school-boy at Dotheboys Hall, then started off in a half trot for the camp, whinnering as he went. We met three others of the five staggering on as best they could, and to each we supplied a little water, but the fifth had bade farewell to the trials and tribulations of the desert journey. When we got back to camp with the animals, tired and worn-out as we were, we enjoyed the consolation of a cooked supper and a good drink of coffee which had been prepared for us. It is wonderful the change in one's temper effected by the comforts of a satisfied stomach. Only a short time before every one was cross and ready to quarrel with the first who would tread on the tail of his coat, but now all were cheerful and sociable. We camped here nearly three days, and by that time our teams had recruited, except those that took the alkali water—they were still weak and drooping.

After three days' rest we traveled on at easy stages for four days, when we became convinced that we had lost our point of compass in the desert, and were now traveling in the direction of Oregon instead of California; but rather than retrace our steps across that one hundred and five miles of desert, we concluded to keep on to the borders of Oregon and take our chances of getting down to California. Better had it been for most of us had we struck our tents and returned to the desert. The fifth night out we camped at the mouth of a deep rock-walled cañon. We had seen no signs of Indians since leaving Humbolt and had become careless, thinking there were none in that part of the country, turning loose the horses without picketing them, and sitting up, telling stories and singing songs, till rather late, when we turned in without a sentry, not having kept one since leaving Salt Lake. Soon all were sound asleep, none dreaming of what was in store for us. Suddenly we were aroused by the ponies rushing into camp, snorting and trembling, and no one could drive them out. We should have known that Indians were around by the actions of the ponies, for they always gave us warning, had we not supposed we were entirely out of the Indian country. But hearing nothing of the other horses and mules, which seemed to be feeding quietly, we came to the conclusion that the ponies had been frightened by wolves, which were plenty in that region. So we went to bed, but only for a brief time, when we were again aroused by yells that could come from none but the throats of redskin devils. In an instant we were up and out. The devils were trying to drive the ponies out of camp. We gave them a warm reception. They then made down among the horses and mules and drove them before them, all the while keeping up their unearthly yells. The Ohio boys were camped more to one side of us, and down nearer where the horses were feeding. Most of them had thrown away their guns, consequently there was no shooting among them, but they ran to secure their horses and mules. When the Indians got among them they let fly a shower of arrows, killing three men dead on the spot, and wounding four more. We followed up, firing after them in the dark, and soon made it so hot for them that they got away with only a part of the stock. When daylight came we mustered about twenty horses all told, including, I am happy to say, the ponies which never left the camp. We buried the three dead comrades in one grave, and cared for the four wounded as best we could. One had three arrows in his body, and could not possibly live but a little while; another had an arrow between the shoulder blades, and it seemed doubtful if he could live. The other two were not so severely wounded, but the arrows were poisoned, so the chances were against them. Then we commenced to pack up, little thinking we would have another attack from the devils, but about eight o'clock they came again in hundreds, showering down on us like hell-hounds, and sending arrows by thousands. The very hills resounded with their yells. There was only one course to pursue, and that was for every man to do the best he could for himself. We rushed for our horses which were close by, but on our way out poor Jim Pierson was struck in the neck by an arrow, just a little ahead of me; he fell, and before he had time to rise to his feet a red devil brained him with a stone tomahawk, and then turned on me; but, thank God, before he had time to commit another such an atrocious and cowardly deed, he got a free leaden passport to join his fathers in the happy hunting grounds. I only wished that poor Jim could have known that his cruel death was so quickly avenged. Those that could reach their horses, did so, and rode for dear life for the mouth of the cañon where the Indians had blocked us off; but we were bound to get to open ground, every one shooting his way through until he got into the open field, when we called the roll and found remaining but nine out

DEATH IN THE CANON.

of twenty-three. We halted for awhile hoping a few more stragglers would come in, but we waited in vain. We loaded our guns and rode back to the mouth of the cañon and fired on them, taking good care that we did not get hemmed in, but the devils were wary of our guns and made for the side hills and skulked behind the rocks. We got one poor fellow who had four arrows in him. He had hidden in a water-hole among some rocks. Others had run down and jumped into the water and tried to hide themselves, but the Indians found them and dispatched them, and such, doubtless, would have been the fate of the one we rescued, had not our second attack frightened them away. He told us he lay in the water with a big pond lily over his face, when the Indians found another who lay not ten feet from him, dragged him out and butchered him, but when they heard our shooting they ran, and then he came out.

We buried them all that afternoon. They were stripped of every article of clothing, and even the poor fellows that we had buried in the morning had been dug up and stripped. We looked around for something they might have left, but there was nothing. God only knew what would become of us; we did not, with nothing left but our arms and old Tige. John See, one of our boys, had put the pack saddle on him, the bag containing our last few pints of flour, and hung the coffee-pot, kettle and frying-pan to the saddle, when the stampede started. Tige followed us through pell-mell, kettle and frying-pan rattling. No doubt he frightened as many Indians as we did. After it was all over, one of the

boys said, "Charlie, you are wounded, too"—and sure
enough, I was. There was an arrow, shaft and all, sticking in my back. It had struck me just over the kidneys,
but had passed through three or four folds of a coarse
woolen shirt, and no doubt that saved my life, but it had
entered so deep into the flesh that it had to be cut out

We stopped there until after dark and then pulled out,
in hopes of deceiving the redskins, which no doubt we did,
and traveled till ten o'clock that night, when we lay down,
taking good care not to be surprised again; then up at
break of day and starting anew, and traveling on till nine
o'clock, when, being perfectly exhausted, we took a rest
and had a consultation as to what to do.

Most of the party were in favor of returning. It was
put to vote and seven were for returning to the sink of the
Humbolt, three in favor of going on through. When
asked where, none could tell. Costler, See, and myself
were for going on. The very ones that had been so determined to take that route, were the ones that now wanted
to go back. I again came to the front. No, I would not
go back. I would not retrace our steps over three
hundred miles, and encounter again those Indians that
had massacred nearly two-thirds of our party, and recross
that desert. Besides, our horses would never stand it, and
if they did we would be farther from any settlement than
we probably were now. They thought we would meet
with others who would let us have provisions. I said we
had none to spare when we were at the sink, and more
than likely those that followed us to that point would be
in like condition; that I firmly believed we were then not

more than two or three hundred miles from Oregon, perhaps not more than one hundred miles; that I had been led off there against my judgment, and now that I was there, all the powers of hell could not turn me back, though every man desert me. Two of the men stood with me. We each had a horse, and old Tige extra, but he was down, and it was plain that he could not last long. We were afraid to kill and eat him, thinking he being poisoned it would be dangerous to us. So we agreed to a fair division of the flour and coffee, for that was all we had. Every man had a pint cup attached to his belt. We found we had just ten pints of flour—just one pint to a man—and six pints of coffee, which we divided into ten parts. The coffee kettle and frying-pan being ours, we claimed it—in fact the flour was ours as well. It was now about noon and time to start. When it came to bidding each other good-by, it was a sad and painful scene. They again urged us to return with them. Costler and See would, I think, had I consented. I told them not to be governed or influenced by me; I was only a boy, but that I had made up my mind not to be led any longer by any one; that I was going through or die in the attempt, even if every man went back. Then they said they would travel with us one or two days longer, if, on finding no change, we would then return with them. I told them I would never retrace our steps; that in my judgment we were approaching the route leading from Oregon to California; that we should strike the road and stand a chance of falling in with emigrants even if we did not strike a settlement in Oregon. That settled it. It had never occurred to them before, and

I must be frank enough to say it had not to me. So, still
an undivided company, we traveled on until five o'clock
that afternoon, camped, built up fires as though we
intended to stay there for the night, but as soon as it was
dark we went on until about ten, when we lay down and
slept till daylight, and then went on until eight or
nine, when we stopped, made coffee and baked our pancake. Our allowance was three spoonfuls of batter each
man—no danger of gout from high living; then after a
little rest we went on till five o'clock, then rested again till
dark, and so on until the fourth day, when in the morning
we found old Tiger had passed in his check. I think there
is a heaven for good horses, and if so, I think "Old Tige"
found a large balance to his credit, and a free range in
green pastures and by clear waters in the celestial realms
where weary and heavy laden horses alone find rest.

John See and I were riding a little ahead of the rest
when we saw a badger and killed it. We thought we had
a prize, and stopped a little earlier that night to cook him.
We boiled him, but when we tried to eat him, one might
as well have undertaken to put his teeth through a piece
of whitleather as through any part of that badger. So
we drank the broth, or rather the water he was boiled in,
for it did not rise to the dignity of broth, even to us famishing men. However, we carried along the boiled badger's remains, riding till the next morning, when the boys
set the badger's corpse boiling again. It was rather a
warm morning, and I lay down in the shade of a tree and
fell asleep. After two or three hours John See said:
"Charlie, get up and have some of your badger." The

shade had shifted and left me with the sun shining full in my face. I felt sick, and the name of badger was enough for me ; my stomach revolted ; I could not even look at the badger, nor could I taste my pancake. One of the party pulled out a twenty dollar gold piece and offered it to me for my pancake. I told him the money was of no use, but if he wanted the cake to take it. But the rest of the boys would not let him take it, and told me to put it in my pocket and keep it until my stomach settled. So I folded it up and put it in my vest pocket and kept it till night when I ate it.

Many, doubtless, who may read this narrative, will be curious to know something how starving men feel, and what are their thoughts, reflections, and even dreams. I can only say to those who have had no such experience, who have been reared and lived in happy homes of plenty and comfort, or rocked in the cradle of luxury and ease, that, speaking for myself, it is utterly impossible to describe my feelings under the circumstances related. No language yet spoken by man has wealth of expression sufficient to convey to one any intelligent or appreciable idea of the emotions, anxieties, distresses, agonies, fears, weariness, despondency and faintness, even unto death, of men so situated. As a slight indication of my mental and physical status under this terrible affliction, I will state that, while riding along alone, the memory of every good dinner I had ever eaten in my life, and every good thing I relished in childhood of my mother's cooking, would come back with such an impressing reality that I seemed to taste it as if still partaking of it. I dreamed of luxurious

meals and cool drafts of water, of tea and coffee, of milk
and cream at home, and awoke only to the sad reality
that it was all a dream. Perhaps, in riding along, one of
the boys would ride up by my side as mentally weak,
weary and faint as myself, and would try to strike up a
little conversation, cheerless, petulant and unhappy as
that of cross and quarreling children, something like this:
"Do you see that gap in the mountain ahead of us?"
"Yes." "Well, do you know when we get up there, I think
the road will turn to the south." Then the sudden and
petulant response· "What in blank do you know about
the road; were you ever there?" "Well, you need not be
so cross about it; I probably know as much about it as
you do." "Well, if you knew so blanked much about the
road, what in blank are you here for, lost in the Sierra
Nevada mountains?" This specimen of unhappy social
intercourse is to show the weakness of both mind and
body among men naturally kind and friendly and imbued
with sympathies resulting from common sorrows. We
had become weak and petulant children. In the midst of
our reflections, perchance a horse would stumble and fall.
"Poor brute," we could only say, "may the Lord pity the
poor horse," for we seemed to have no mercy. These unhappy feelings were apt to possess us generally about an
hour after eating our little cake, when our stomachs were
gnawing the reason and judgment out of our brains, as
then we were weak and stomach-sick, but agreeable
enough to each other generally.

CHAPTER VIII.

ANOTHER COMRADE KILLED—ELEVEN DEAD INDIANS—PROVISIONS GONE
—SHALL A HORSE BE KILLED—WAGON TRAIL DISCOVERED—HOPE
REVIVED — GREAT REJOICING — OREGON PARTY — RESCUED — THE
WOMEN—MUSH AND MILK—PRICE OF PROVISIONS—YANKEE DOODLE
BEEF—CUTTING OUT THE ARROW—INDIAN CAMP SURPRISED—THE
CAPTAIN'S HOPEFUL SON — PULLING THE CAPTAIN'S TOOTH — THE
QUACK DOCTOR.

ON the fifth day after the boys were killed, when we
had camped and made our coffee and cakes, one of
the party's horse having gone lame, he thought he would
walk on ahead and lead his horse, and we would overtake
him. We all tried to persuade him not to go alone, but
he was determined and we were not in the best of humor;
but go he would and did, and we said no more. We remained about two hours after he left, and then started.
After about two hours, John See and I being about
two hundred yards ahead of the rest, we heard a terrible
noise, and listened, and at once came to the conclusion that
there were Indians ahead. I held the horses while See
went cautiously and looked around a bend of the spur of
a hill. He soon returned, and the other boys coming up
and seeing John's movements, knew something was not
right, and he reported what he had seen. We left the
horses with the wounded man and crawled around the

point, when a strange sight presented itself. There were at least thirty Indians around a big fire having a high old time, yelling, howling, laughing, others feasting. We got around the point, unobserved by them, and within a hundred and fifty yards, when we all took deliberate aim and fired, then rushed upon them, yelling as loud as any of those devils ever did, and at the same time firing our revolvers at them. Only two of us, however, had Colt's revolvers; others had "Allen's pepper-boxes," as the early style of revolvers were called. The Indians were as much taken by surprise as we were a few days before, and ran for their lives as we did, that is, those that had lives to run for, for some of them bit the dust, and some that were not dead but only wounded when we reached them, immediately started on their journey to the happy hunting ground of Manitou the Mighty. On looking around we soon found the lifeless body of Freddy, the only name we knew him by, his clothes stripped off and fourteen arrows in him. His gun lay by his side, discharged, and the stock broken. Near him lay three redskins, which testified to the severity of the conflict and the heroism of our companion. We buried the poor boy as well as we could, and left with only the slight consolation that there were eleven less Indians in this world than an hour before.

We traveled that night without stopping, as we formerly had, and did not camp till ten in the morning. Our provisions were now all gone, no flour, and only coffee enough to make two more drinks. Our reasons for not killing a horse before were, if we did so it would put at least three of us on foot, and that would retard our progress, and that so long as the flour lasted we had determined not to kill one.

Now the question presented itself, whose horse was to be killed. My "Billey" was in the best condition, and some proposed to kill him. I objected, and the matter was dropped until we halted the next morning, when the horse killing bill was again offered in council. I offered to cast lots, and if it fell to my horse I would accept the result in silence, but not without. Blank, the man who had so much to say, when we left the Humbolt, about the boy that had just left his mother, spoke up and said he was not going to pick bones when there was plenty of meat, and took his gun to shoot Billey. Upon that I took my pistol out and stepped up to him, telling him that as sure as he shot that horse I would give him an immediate interview with his Maker. For that he did not seem to feel prepared, and desisted. All the rest were against him, saying that I only demanded what was fair for all. Then we all agreed to defer the killing till afternoon, camp early, and kill and have a good feast. So we started with that understanding and traveled until about two o'clock. While we were on the lookout for a good place to camp and kill, we came around a short turn, where, to our great surprise and joy, we came upon a fresh wagon trail, not more than three days old—a very fresh track to us.

Had an angel from Heaven come down and invited us to dine in the meads of Asphodel, he could not have been received with greater rejoicing or with more grateful hearts than was the sight of that simple wagon trail, three days old, in the rocky recesses of the Sierra Nevada.

mountains. We shouted and laughed, shook hands, yes, and cried. Even good Blank came to me and asked me to forgive him, showered compliments on me, said I was a good boy, that he never intended to shoot Billey, that it was a good thing it so turned out, as otherwise we should have had to kill a horse and that would have put us back, and now we were sure to be all right. And as for myself, I would have forgiven anybody or anything but an Indian. We followed that trail until we reached their camp of the night before. Then we lay down, but were up again in the morning betimes, and soon struck their last camp, when we felt sure of overtaking the party within three hours. But our horses began to lag, and we were so worn out and weak that when we got off we had to be helped on again. Not one had strength to mount his horse without assistance. The arrow wound in my back was greatly inflamed and very sore. I had done nothing for it except that the boys used to wash it; and as for the other wounded man, how he ever stood it to ride as he did and live, has always been a mystery to me. He had four arrow wounds in his body, and was red all over with inflammation, and swollen as full as his skin could hold, and so weak he could hardly sit on his horse, but he bore it all without a murmur. Two or three of the horses began to stop and refuse to go, and we were compelled to leave them. It was then thought best for those who could, to ride ahead and get the train to stop. Costler, See and myself went and overtook them just as the party had rested for the day. As soon as they heard our pitiful story, they, like true mountaineers, volunteered to go back and meet those we had left behind. A light wagon was hitched up and a small party of horsemen galloped back, followed by the wagon, to bring the wounded man in, and as for me, I began to think I was in Paradise. They proved to be a party of emigrants from Oregon bound for California, and taking all their stock with them. They had cows, calves, pigs, sheep, and even hens and turkeys, moving with their outfit for the new gold fields.

No sooner had our party been brought in than the women of the emigrant party, having learned of our starving condition, with that natural propensity that prompts the heart of woman, set about the work of cooking, each trying to surpass the other in generous acts. I was lying on the ground in front of a tent when an elderly woman came out and invited me into her tent and gave me a bowl of mush and milk. I never tasted anything so good, and it is needless to say I was not long in putting it out of sight, and then, like Oliver Twist, asked for more. But the old lady refused me. I told her I had money, that I did not want it for nothing. It was not money, she said, but that too much was not good for me. I could not understand the dear old lady's philosophy. I had had nothing to eat for a long time, and was now where there was plenty, was hungry and willing to pay, and why couldn't she let me have it? Weak in mind almost as in body, like a disappointed and unhappy child, I got up to leave her tent, feeling that, after all, she was a stingy old creature, unwilling to give a starving man only so little, even when he was willing to pay for it. But just as I had stepped outside, up came another bowl of the delicious mush and milk. The old lady stood by quietly looking on, and when I had finished it, she said in a most gentle and motherly tone, "Now, young man, you are welcome to more and all you want." She knew better than I did how to treat the empty stomach of a long fasting and famishing man.

The wounded man and all our party being in, the devoted women had something of every kind they had cooked, and it was brought out and every one invited to eat, which we all did, though some afterwards paid dearly for their lack of judgment and excesses. No one ever saw poor fellows in such misery as the most of us were in. I was not as bad as the rest, for the mush and milk administered by the sagacious and prudent old lady had prepared my stomach for the severer ordeal it had to undergo in receiving an undue quantity of bacon and eggs and hot biscuit, just the food our stomachs were unprepared for, and under the cravings of which we had neither judgment nor prudence.

The Oregonians very generously offered to lay over a day that we might rest ourselves and horses, which were as much worn out as we were. They told us Indians were ahead of us and that it would be better for us to travel with them, an invitation we most gladly accepted. They always kept out scouts to look out for the noble Indian, and woe to the red devil that crossed their path. They told us that the tribe that killed so many of our party, were the Goose Lake Indians. That those we were among now were an Upper California tribe, and that in all probability those that killed Freddy were of the same tribe, as it was far south of the Goose Lake country, and the lake tribe was not likely to encroach upon the Feather river tribes. They held over two whole days for our party to recruit, then traveled by short and easy stages, starting at eight in the morning and camping about two in the afternoon, making only about fifteen miles a day, which was a great relief to our poor fagged and jaded horses. But judge of our surprise when we came to buy provisions of them. Only think, ye who never paid more than three or four cents a pound for flour by the barrel or sack in the scarcest times, of paying a dollar a pound for everything, flour, meat, coffee, and even salt. The captain of the party was a shrewd man and a money maker. He was well to do, and had plenty of stock and money. He had already been in California and had done well, and knew just what he was doing now, and what would be the outcome of his present enterprise. He offered to buy our horses at fifty dollars a head, and let us ride them—that is, if we would remain with them. Of course before we got in the proceeds of the horses, the fifty pounds of provisions would have been eaten up. Some of the boys were compelled to sell as they had no money; and probably we would all have been necessitated to do the same had it not been for a lucky circumstance that happened. He was very obliging; anything we wanted that he had we could have, of course by paying a dollar a pound. We wanted some beef, and he offered to kill a fat one if we would take one hundred and fifty pounds; it was only to oblige us. We consented to take it; but judge of our surprise when the fat beef turned out to be a little runt of a nine months heifer. It reminded me of the song descriptive of the beef that Yankee Doodle killed, which took two men to hold it up while Mr. Doodle knocked it down. For beef this poor little heifer took the cake. But what were we to do? We must have meat, and had to have it; besides, we were not very particular, any tasted good, and such appetites as we had were uncontrollable; we were eating all the time, and it is no wonder that some or all of us were sick. The poor fellow that was wounded had to be carried in the wagon, getting worse every day, and his wounds a sight to behold. The Oregonians were very good to him, especially the women, who looked after him and dressed his wounds, and were as kind to him as if he had been a brother. But he had now become peevish as a child, and grumbled and fretted and almost seemed ungrateful in return for their kind care. I never saw such a change in anyone in my life. Doubtless he suffered greatly from the jar and jolting of the wagon; besides, I think he knew he could not live, and that still more disturbed his weakened mind. He lived only till we got into Lessen's, and died during the night—was found dead in the morning. He was the sixteenth of our party killed by the Indians.

My own wound was now progressing as well as could be expected. As the arrow had been cut out, the wound bled freely. No doubt the poison was drawn out so largely as to be ineffective, and I applied some salve that my brother, the doctor, gave me, which proved beneficial. On the whole, it was just as well that old George drank the brandy, for otherwise it would have fallen into the hands of the Indians, and the quinine too, had we not, after dis-

covering George's affection for the jug, carried the other
medicines on our persons—Costler the quinine and I the
salve—thus saving it in our retreat that fatal morning.
One evening, after camping, a scout of the Oregon party
rode in and reported a party of Indians camped about five
miles ahead, about twenty in number; that having seen
signs of the band he had followed on unobserved until he
found them camped; that they had evidently been there
some time, as they had built huts. All were up in arms in
a few minutes, and ready to start for them. The women
were as much excited as the men. But the captain put a
stop to their haste; told them the better plan would be
to wait till night and crawl carefully out and bag the
whole party. His plan was adopted, and guns were
cleaned and ammunition looked after. It was arranged
that some should remain with the women and children,
and the rest to start about eleven o'clock, surround their
camp, and at a signal rush in and surprise the ferocious
native. Three of our party volunteered—there was no
lack of volunteers, the trouble was, all wanted to go,
which would leave the home-guard too small. But the
women were not afraid to remain alone; they wanted the
"red devils rubbed out," as they expressed it. While the
preparation was being made for the raid upon the Indian
camp, an amusing little incident occurred. The captain had
a little dumpy stub of a boy, some six or seven years old,
about as thick as he was long, who came stubbing up to
his father, saying: "Fader, fader, I want you to buy me
a wyfle." "What do you want a rifle for, my son?" said
the father. "I want to shoot the Ingins," replied the pre-

cocious son and heir, emphasizing his answer with one of his father's most profane curses. "That's right, my son," said his father, "I'll buy you a rifle," and his eye beamed with fatherly pride. He was proud of his son's speech, and, doubtless, regarded him as a rising young Norval. I think if that boy had cut down all the cherry trees in Oregon, and then lied about it, the old man would have cheerfully gone his bail and carried up the case. If the biography of that father has ever been written and placed in the libraries of Oregon, it will probably be found that he was not a descendant of a Puritan family.

It was midnight when we started, and half-past two when we arrived in sight of the Indian camp. Their fires were burning dimly. The captain ordered a halt, and then he crawled up a little nearer and reconnoitered. There were eighteen of our party. The captain returned, placed the men about equal distance apart around the camp, and ordered each to crawl silently to within about one hundred yards of the camp, and there lie perfectly quiet till a signal from him, when we should come down upon them. It was understood that the raid was to be made just at break of day, or when light enough to see that none escaped. Judging from the systematic manner in which he went about the work, I think it was not the first Indian camp he had surprised. I had lain full three-quarters of an hour when the signal was given by one most unearthly yell from the captain. The prime object thereof was to bring the redskins out of their tents. In an instant every man was on his feet, running and yelling at the top of his voice, and in less time than it takes to tell the story, twenty-seven wild and ferocious Indians were changed into harmless spirits of the air, never more to take the war-path or surprise and slaughter a party of emigrants.

Some may think it was a cruel and unmanly proceeding, but had those who think so been situated as we were—whose companions had been massacred before our eyes; whose dead of a few days before still lay naked and unburied in the cañon, and those we hastily buried exhumed and stripped of their grave clothes, driven to the extreme verge of starvation; saved from death only by the mere chance of having fallen in with another party; standing guard by night, and sending out scouts by day to look out for a ferocious enemy, as the man-eating tiger lurking near villages and isolated homes in Hindustan is watched for and hunted by the natives—I think, if happily they survived to return, it would be with modified views of the emigrants' dealings with the plundering and murderous tribes of the interior of the continent in the year of grace '49.

Still, if anyone thinks otherwise, and believes that a free and roving tribe, uncontrolled by military force, can be humanized and civilized by any process known to civilized or Christianized man, I nevertheless would warn him not to risk his person among them. Powder, not prayer, is their only civilizer. You cannot manage him by reasoning with him and persuading him, as the wag said he controlled his vicious and cantankerous mule. Nothing will convert an Indian like convincing him that you are his superior, and there is but one process by which even that can be done, and that is to shut off his wind. I never knew but one "truly good" Indian, and he was dead. I have heard considerable romance, from persons inexperienced, about the brave and noble red man, but I never yet have met one. All I have ever known have been cowardly and treacherous, never attack like men, but crawl upon you, three or four to one, and shoot you down, as they did sixteen of our party in the cañon. Then why not attack them, not wait to be attacked by them, and then only in self-defense take, perhaps, one of their worthless lives? In all modern civilized warfare, to surprise the enemy and kill, if they do not surrender, is the climax of military renown. The world applauds, congress promotes, parliament does likewise, graciously voting the hero of the hour, at the same time, a little hundred thousand pounds and a dukedom, and even bishops, priests and clergy offer prayers and incense to divine Providence for the delivery of their equally civilized and equally honorable and patriotic enemy into their hands! But if a party of emigrants surprise and annihilate a band of Indians, who, perhaps, only the day before had murdered every man, woman and child of a large train, and spattered the wagon wheels with the brains of babes, why, the Christian world holds up its hands in breathless horror. But what is the difference? The Indian is the emigrant's enemy. If the emigrant gets the advantage, why should he not take it, for most surely the Indian will? I do not believe in wanton cruelty to the Indian, but when you are in a country where you know he is your enemy, and is not only waiting his chance but looking out for his opportunity, why not cut him down, as otherwise he most surely will you?

Nearly two hundred years ago the peaceful settlers of New England had a mournful experience with the local tribes of Indians, less ferocious, it is believed, than the tribes of the interior of the present day. The well known history of Mrs. Dustin of Haverill, Massachusetts, who, in 1697, was carried off with her infant, only a week old, and her nurse, is an impressive instance of savagery and the heroism and glorious triumph of a noble and distressed woman. She was taken from her bed, half dressed, and, without shoes or stockings, exposed to the cold March winds. They took her northward by canoes, up the Merrimac to a point near Concord, New Hampshire. They had killed the babe at the outset. Here they rested for the night with an Indian family. Getting some intimation that they were soon to suffer shocking cruelty, Mrs. Dustin resolved to attempt escape, and laid her plans with her nurse, Mary Neff, and a boy prisoner, named Leonardson. At midnight, when the savages were asleep, Mrs. Dustin, the nurse and boy killed the Indians, took off their scalps, scuttled all the canoes but one to prevent pursuit, and set off down the river for Haverill. They reached home with the scalps as evidence of their prowess, and then found safety in Boston.

Happily now there is a little light in the east on the subject of the justifiable treatment of the savage by the modern emigrant, for, as recently as 1874, the humane and gentle descendants of the Pilgrims have delineated in imperishable marble the thrilling story of Mrs. Dustin. A monument to her and her companions has been erected near the scene of the tragedy. On a pedestal, bearing appropriate inscriptions, is a statue of Mrs. Dustin, represented as holding a tomahawk in her right hand and a bunch of scalps in the other. The arms are bare to the shoulders. The right hand is raised in the attitude of striking. The hair is loose and flowing, and the body is enclosed in graceful drapery. One of the inscriptions gives the names of the two women and the boy, as follows: "HANNAH DUSTIN, MARY NEFF, AND SAMUEL LEONARDSON, MARCH 30, 1697, MIDNIGHT."

It may possibly be inferred from this digression touching the general traits of the Indian, that I am not an ardent admirer of the character, manners and customs of Mr. Lo. I confess I did intend so to be understood.

When we returned to our camp, about six o'clock in the morning, all was excitement, and everyone wanted to hear the news and its minutest particular, and each one had to relate it to another, as there was no war correspondent in our party, nor a newspaper reporter on that night's battle-field. It was a day of general rejoicing in our camp, and of course no traveling, as we had been out all night and wanted sleep. The captain caught a cold which resulted in a jumping toothache, and he was raving and rearing mad. John See asked him why he did not have it pulled. "How can I have it pulled?" said he. "We have no doctor; besides, it is a double tooth." See told him we had a doctor in our party, and came to me, saying, "Charlie, I have a job for you." "What is it?" said I. "To pull the captain's tooth." "Why," said I, "I never pulled a

tooth in my life." "It don't matter," said John, "you
have got to pull his, for I told him you were a doctor and
a first-rate hand at pulling teeth, so you have got to pull
his or make me out a liar." "Why," said I, "I might break
his jaw." "Damn the odds," said he, "you've got to pull
it, and, what is more, make him pay for it." "What!" said
I, "shall I charge five dollars?" "Five dollars be
blanked," said John, "don't charge him less than twenty
dollars." "He charges us a dollar a pound for his old
musty flour, and surely any doctor would charge twenty
pounds of flour for pulling a tooth." Well, John persuaded me to make the attempt. It so happened I had a
pair of those old-fashioned "turnkeys" doctors formerly
used, which were given me by my brother, the doctor, in
Illinois, when I started. They looked more like a "cant-
hook" used for rolling logs in a saw-mill than like the
instrument now used by dentists for extracting molars.

In a short time the captain came in great agony, holding
his hand firmly against his jaw. "Doctor," said he, "I
want you to pull a tooth for me." With the gravity of
a bona fide M. D., I said, "Let me look at it." I looked at
it and pronounced it a very bad one, and advised him not
to have it pulled. I knew he was in such agony he would
have it out any way, and my advice was only a professional ruse, partly to impress his mind with the certain
belief that he was in the hands of an experienced and
prudent surgeon, but more especially for the reason that
if, perchance, I should break his jaw, or carry away a
portion of his head, I could plead to an action for mal-
practice that he had been forewarned of the danger of the

operation, but persisted therein against my advice. John was standing off a short distance, gesticulating for me to go ahead. So I got the captain seated on the ground, with his head between my knees, got out my lance (jack-knife) and commenced chopping and digging away around the gum of the tooth. The women all ran away as soon as I commenced to mutilate the patient's mouth with the lancet. John came forward as my student and assistant and handed me the turnkeys. I got them hooked on at last, but considerable time and not a little professional skill were expended in manipulating the ponderous hook and nicely attaching it to the throbbing tooth. I then straightened myself up into a position a little more dignified and gave the instrument a slight twist, just to be sure it was on firmly, which made him wince so that I began to lose courage and would willingly have given up the job, to the ruin of my professional standing, had I not just at that moment caught the eye of John, who gave an approving, nod and wink and whose facial expressions and gesticulations seemed to say, "Courage, boy, out with it." I gave a final twist and jerk, and out flew the tooth and struck the ground a good two yards distant. The captain jumped up and discharged a few mouthfuls of blood, and assured me that he had never before in all his life had a tooth pulled so skillfully. I assured him in return that in all my professional experience I had never encountered such a tenacious and resisting molar. He expressed great satisfaction, said he felt greatly relieved. So did I. He asked how much was the charge. I again assumed the typical professional air and gravity of coun-

PULLING THE CAPTAIN'S TOOTH.

THE "DOCTOR'S" FAME AND PRACTICE.   111

tenance and said, twenty dollars. He handed me one of
the very gold pieces we had given him for twenty pounds
of musty flour, and handed it over freely, without haggle
or complaint. Henceforth my reputation as a doctor
was made. Every woman in the camp and train consulted
me about her every ache and pain. The children too, they
said, had been neglected; they had always lived so far
away from a doctor, and now that they had one right
among them, they were bound to make up for past neglect.

My practice was now becoming large. My consulting
hours when we were traveling were after supper. Besides,
I had to compound many medicinal remedies. Fortunately for me, I was provided with a good stock of search-
ing and raking pills that were sure to do their work.
Then I had some calomel, but that I did not thoroughly
understand, but administered it very prudently, and
always followed it up by a dose of those never failing pills,
so I lost not a patient from an overdose of calomel. As
my practice was increasing rapidly, it stood me in hand
to be careful lest my stock of medicines would run out; and
as a preventive of such possibility, I used some of the
flour I had bought of the captain for a dollar a pound and
prescribed it in some chronic cases at two dollars a prescription, exclusive of my professional charge for the visit.
The quinine held out well and was useful and effective in
malarial regions, and in cold and rainy weather. However,
my practice was not wholly confined to medicine; my
surgical skill as well was sought for. One Oregonian had
a little lump growing on the side of his neck, a little
larger than a good sized bean. I had seen my brother cut

one out only a short time before I left, from the neck of a
Norwegian. The man came to me. I pronounced it a
growing tumor. That was enough; the whole camp was
talking about it. Of course I was asked how large it
would grow, and how long it would be about it. I shook
my head, and with slowness of speech and gravity of manner, said that would depend on how long the dangerous
thing was suffered to remain before it was cut out—which
it would have to be, sooner or later. He asked what I
would charge to perform the operation. I said, fifty dollars. He concluded to have it done. So at the camping
time he came, and I pinched the skin underneath the lump,
slit the skin, and out popped the little hard bean. I dressed
the wound, putting on some salve and telling him to keep
it bound up and be careful about his diet, or it might
cost him his life. That was a master stroke for me—a
learned doctor with such a practice, a skillful surgeon, and
only seventeen years old! It was certainly unprecedented
in the cañons of the Sierra Nevada mountains. But my
professional eminence must be credited not alone to the
desperate emergencies of our situation, but largely, if not
wholly, to John See as an advertiser. He blew my horn.
Vive l'humbug!

THE FIRST CAMP
IN THE
GOLD REGION

CHAPTER IX.

A Prospecting Party—Generosity—Lessen's Ranch—Parting with the Oregonians—Near the Gold Fields—Sensations—Dinner in Camp—First Day's Digging—Mountain Fever—Mining Operations —Grizzly Bear—Lurking Indians—Finding Ohio Boys—Marysville—Yuba City—High Prices.

WE had now been in the Oregon train about two weeks. One evening, a little before sundown, we discovered a party of seven coming down the mountain, all with pack mules, which we, of course, took to be emigrants. Our party again getting reduced in flour and other provisions, I went to the captain for more. He asked what we were willing to pay. Costler spoke up and told him we were willing to pay a dollar a pound as before. "No," the captain said, "I want one and a half," for the party we saw coming were sure to be out of provisions, and that was what he should charge them, and he could not let us have it for less. That settled it. Costler was a high-tempered little fellow, and blustered considerably in his diplomacy, and told the captain he was not going to be robbed—he not considering that in my medical and surgical practice I had fleeced our good Oregon friends as much as they had robbed us in unconscionable charges. In fact, considering my professional income as medical director of the train, I felt that flour at a dollar and a half a pound was moderate and reasonable. By this time the strangers had arrived, and proved to be prospectors who had been out on the west branch of the north fork of Feather river, and were now on their return, with plenty of provisions they did not need. When they were told the extortionary charges we had been and were necessitated to submit to, they offered us all they had, only reserving enough to carry them through to Sacramento. They told us we were only about fifty miles from Lessen's. It elevated our spirits higher than the top of the highest mountain to think that in three days more we would be there. We could hardly realize it, but so it was. Twenty-four had started only a few days before, and now only nine were alive, and one of them past all hopes of recovery—soon to be dead and buried. In three days more we arrived at Lessen's ranch on the Sacramento river, about one hundred and twenty-five miles above Sacramento city. The next morning we parted with our Oregon friends. I had a very pressing invitation to go with them and follow my profession, but I declined, telling them that I had come out to try my fortune in the gold fields, and if I failed in that, there would be time for me to turn again to my profession. The women thought it was a pity such a clever young doctor as I was should go digging. Before I left, the captain gave me fifty dollars for a bottle of quinine in solution—a pretty fair profit; but when one comes to look at it, there was not so much profit as there was on fifty pounds of flour at the prices charged.

Costler, See and myself now started off for the nearest

gold diggings, which, we were told, were at Butte creek, about thirty-three miles distant. Our first day's travel was to Newell's ranch, twenty-five miles distant. Newell had crossed the plains with Fremont, in 1848, and had started a ranch there, and seemed to be in a fair way of making a fortune. He was an Irish-American, and a first-rate fellow. We stopped with him over night, and he gave us a great deal of information. He said there were a few parties up the creek, eight miles away, on Reece's bar, and some of them were doing well. Others were cutting a channel to turn the creek so they could work the bed of the stream, anticipating fortunate results therefrom.

Now we were within only eight miles of where men were actually getting gold. I am unable to express our mental sensations—exaltation of spirit for triumphs achieved, and expectancy on the verge of realization. For over a year visions of gold fields had fairly bewildered my youthful brain, and now here was I, right where, in twenty-four hours, I would see men digging out the golden nuggets and sifting the precious sands in the beds of ancient rivers. I did not sleep that night nor did my two companions. We talked and planned and built castles in the air all night. But, alas! many of those fine castles were doomed to fall to the ground. In the morning we sold our horses to Newell for seventy-five dollars a head—two ponies and the horse I bought of the Crow Indians for a pint of well watered brandy and a pint of sugar. In return we bought of him a ham, at a dollar a pound, ten pounds of sugar, twenty pounds of flour, ten pounds of jerked beef, some coffee, one pick, at eight dollars, and one shovel at the same price, a

tin-pan at six dollars, and two pair of blankets at sixteen dollars a pair. When we got the stuff packed we
found we had more than we could carry, though many
times since I have carried more myself alone. But we
were weak and worn out, so we thought we would try to
buy Billey back. But no, he would not sell him, but offered
to lend him to us to take our things up, telling us we
would soon want more stuff, and that we need not be in
a hurry to return him, that if we stopped with him we
could always have a horse to take our provisions to the
mines.

We started at last, thinking Newell was the best fellow
we ever met, and I never had any occasion to think otherwise. It was about seven o'clock in the morning. Our
hearts were full of hopes and fond expectations. We
traveled up the creek about four miles, and had just
entered where the stream commenced to cañon the banks,
which were so thick with a growth of scrub we could
hardly see through to the steam, when we heard men talking, stones rattling, and the sound of the picks. We listened, and at length ventured into the scrub, and looking
through saw four men working, talking and laughing.
We stood for some minutes with beating hearts. We
had at last seen with our own eyes what we had so
long wished for, and for which we had crossed the
continent. Men actually digging for gold. We stood and
conversed in whispers. Finally we mustered up courage
and went through the scrubs to them, when they saluted
us with, "Good day, captains, where from?" We told
them we had arrived from across the plains only the

day before, and had never seen any gold fields. They at once invited us to their camp, which was on the opposite side of the creek from where our pony was, one man going with John See to show him a crossing, Martin Costler and myself going with the other three to the camp. Dinner was soon on the way. We had to give them all the news and a full account of our journey, which they listened to with the greatest interest. They had come around the Horn. There was no work for them that afternoon. They would not hear of our going any farther that day, and would not allow us to cook any of our provisions. That night they told us they were prospecting the creek by putting in what they called a wing-dam, and if we liked we could go to work with them and all share alike.

We accepted their proposition and the next morning went to work putting in the wing-dam, which is constructed by building a wall of stone diagonally about half way across the stream, then fill in with earth to dam the water back and throw the current to the opposite side, then, in like manner, down the stream. When this is accomplished, the river bed within the enclosure is accessible from the surface to the bed-rock. The dirt is then tried from top to bottom with a tin pan, or gold dish, as it is called among miners. Sometimes gold is obtained all through the dirt, but generally the richest is found at the bottom. Well, we worked two days and sunk a hole to the bed-rock without obtaining satisfactory results—that is, so the parties we were working with said. Our spirits went down about ten degrees below zero, and we made up our minds to quit and go farther up the stream to a place called Reece's Bar. They told us we must not get discouraged at not dropping on it at once; that we might have to try without success for a long time, especially as we were beginners; that gold-digging was a trade that one had to learn the same as any other, but that if we went to Reece's Bar we were sure to get gold there in the side of the hill, but that we could do nothing without a cradle. What we wanted a cradle for was more than any of us could tell—we had no children to rock. But, however, we started the next morning, rather down in the mouth, especially Costler, though John seemed to take it a little better. It was four miles up the creek, and on rather a rough road. Some twenty or thirty men were working there, and had cut a race, blasted the rock, dug out a new channel for the creek, built a dam across the stream and turned it into the race or new channel to enable them to work the original bottom of the stream.

We found the men here equally as hospitable and friendly as the party below. Dinner we must have with them, and no excuse was admissible. After dinner one of them showed us where we could set in and make wages. It was in the side of a hill, digging up the surface, grass, roots and all, and carrying it on our backs some fifty or more yards to the stream to wash. He showed us how to wash in a tin dish, but told us we would have to have a cradle—there, again, came up that mysterious and to us useless cradle. I told him I did not need a cradle; that I was an unmarried man of reputable character and, therefore, could not be the father of children; that I had not even been courting any young lady in the east. He laughed heartily at my simplicity and explained to us the form and use of what the miners call a cradle or rocker. It is a box about three feet and a half long, the bottom about sixteen inches wide, its sides about the same in height, the upper half having a strip or riffle across the bottom about an inch thick, and one on the lower end. The top has a hopper about sixteen inches square, with a sheet iron screen full of holes punched about an inch apart and about half an inch in diameter. Underneath the hopper is a canvas apron fixed on a slide set so as to pitch back to the upper side or back end of the cradle, at an angle of about fifteen degrees. Underneath the cradle are attached two rockers, like a child's cradle, with two little iron spikes, and also a strip with two holes in the centre for the spikes, and on the back end is a handle to rock the cradle. It is set on an incline, towards the tail or lower end, of about half an inch to the foot—now you are ready for rocking out the gold. The process is to put into the hopper about half a bucket of dirt, having a dipper holding a quart of water, commence rocking the cradle steadily, at the same time pouring in the water regularly so as to have a steady stream running off. One has to learn to do three things at once—rock, dip and pour—which is difficult at first to do, as all boys know who have experimented on only two simultaneous acts—scratching the head with one hand and spatting the chest with the other.

Our new friend told us he had a cradle he was not using, which he would lend us until he wanted to use it himself, which was very kind in him, especially as one was worth about forty dollars. He brought it and set it for us,

panned out two or three dishes of dirt, told us we had a
first-rate prospect, and then had me try my hand. I made
a very poor hand at it. I found I could not even do two
things at once—could not rock and dip at the same time.
The others then tried it, but did no better, and perhaps not
quite so well as I did; so I was tolled off to rock the
cradle. See carried down the dirt in a fifty pound flour
sack, and Costler dug up the surface and picked out
the coarse stones. When our friend got us to work all
right he left, telling us to call him when we wanted to
clean out the rocker. We commenced work at half past
two o'clock, but in two hours Costler gave out—he could
stand it no longer—and as for myself, if he had not stopped
as he did, I should have ceased rocking, for I was completely
played out. We called our new friend, who came and
cleaned up for us, we, all the while, looking on with the
greatest anxiety. When he got it panned down my spirits
dropped; still he kept panning out the sand until I
thought he was going to pan it all away. At last he got
through, and there looked to me to be a very small
amount of precious settlings for so much work. He told
us that it was first-rate; that if he had thought that it
had been any where near so good he would have worked
it himself. That rather frightened us; perhaps he would
take the cradle away from us. However, he took the little
results of our rockings down to his camp, dried it, and
put it into a blower to blow out the sand. Now I was
sure it was all gone, for he kept blowing and shaking and
blowing again, until I thought the last particle was bound
to go. He then poured it into his gold scales and weighed

it. Judge of our surprise when he told us that there were just two ounces, two and a half pennyweights, or thirty-five dollars worth. We could hardly believe him, and yet felt that our fortunes were secured. See wanted to go to work again that afternoon, but poor Costler was too much worn out, and I was not much better. The next day we were at it bright and early, but we all fagged and often had to stop and rest, and by the middle of the afternoon we shut down. Our friend showed us how to clean out the cradle every hour and leave the dirt in the dish, and at noon came and panned it off for us. That day we had five ounces and five pennyweights, or eighty-four dollars.

The next morning Costler was as crazy as a loon—the mountain fever had attacked him. What to do we did not know. I had medicine, but when it came to practicing on a friend that was really sick, it was a different thing from practicing on my Oregon patients who needed not a physician. But the poor fellow had to have something, and so I tried to do the best I could. I began by giving a whopping dose of calomel, followed up by as large a dose of pills; then quinine came in, but nothing seemed to quiet his brain or check his fever. He raved and talked all sorts of nonsense—sometimes he was fighting Indians, and one of us had to stop with him constantly. I kept repeating my routine of prescriptions, not knowing whether I was doing right or wrong. After six days I could stand it no longer, and having been told that there was a doctor about ten miles away, I left See with him and went to see the doctor, found him, stated the case and what I had done. He listened to me in profound silence and with closed eyes, as though he was taking a mental review of all the cases in the books from Esculapius or Galen down to that hour. Finally he opened his eyes, coughed, cleared his throat, and with a grave and sedate countenance told me that the course of treatment I had pursued was the correct one, that in his opinion it was a very stubborn and doubtful case; that if he went to see him his charge would be one hundred dollars that he was just as well satisfied with my diagnosis as if he had seen the patient; that he should treat him the same as I had. I asked him his fee for the consultation. He said, "O, nothing at all, perhaps he should sometimes have a stubborn case and need my counsel." That settled it with me; I knew then he was an impostor. I then went to the store there and bought a bottle of brandy for which I paid sixteen dollars, and then started back as fast as Billey could carry me, and I did not get back any too soon. Costler's fever had broken and he had a sinking spell. We both thought he was going to die, and very soon. I thought to try the brandy and got some, mixed with water, down him, when he revived, and one of us staid with him all the time, never leaving him, every now and then giving him a spoonful of the brandy and water, and quinine in grain doses every three hours. The men on the bar were very kind and sat up with him nights, and were willing to do anything for him. At last he began to recover, so that I could leave him. I now began to feel uneasy about keeping Billey so long, and went down to Newell's to apologize and explain. He said he had heard that there was a man on the bar that could not live, but that he had one of the cleverest young doctors attending him. Upon my inquiry as to who told him, he said it was Dr. Bliss from the Springs, the same old humbug I had been to see. I bought Billey back for one hundred dollars, twenty-five more than I sold him for. I found we must have a horse and that Billey would suit us better than any other we could get. I bought more provisions and returned. See was working away, but Costler was nowhere to be found. I called to See to know what had become of him. He told me he had just left him, that he worked a little while and then went to see if he wanted anything, and then returned to work again. We looked everywhere and called for him, but no answer, when we began to think he had crawled to the dam and had fallen in. There was a deep gorge close by and a spring of ice-cold water in it, and as one of us was running past it a noise was heard, and looking around, there lay Costler by the spring, with nothing on but his shirt, sticking his head in the water and then shaking it like a Newfoundland dog. We carried him back; he had become so emaciated that one could carry him like a child. He had got a relapse and was as bad as ever. I gave up all hopes of saving him, but was determined to try. I treated much as before, only in smaller doses. I got some arrow-root at Newell's, but he would not take it, accused us of trying to poison him, called us everything that was bad, and, although a very religious man, swore at us like a pirate. We had an awfully trying time with him; but at last he began to recover, and after about three weeks got so we could leave him and both go to work. We still continued to do pretty well at the cradle, and had we been able to do a full day's work, we would have made from forty to fifty dollars a day. Soon Costler got so he could get around, but he was so cross that he was very disagreeable. He got it into his head that we must get out of that place. See and I opposed it, but that did not satisfy him, go we should; and finally, to gratify his whim we consented to go across to Feather river, a distance of about thirty-five miles; packed up Billey, offered to pay for the use of the cradle, thanked the party for their kindness, and departed for the main fork of the Feather river. Costler was not equal to the journey, and before we had gone four miles we had to load him onto the horse. He rode ten miles to the Springs, where I had consulted the doctor, and there we had to lay over for him three days, and at last reached Long's Bar. See and I prospected around for three or four days and thought we would set in on Morris' ravine, about a mile and a half distant. Costler went over with us; but no, that place did not suit him, and he wasn't going to stop there. To be sure it was not so good as the place we had left, but it was better to stop there than to be running around. No, he wanted to go to Sacramento and us to go with him. See, I think, would have gone if I had not told him I had lost time enough in running around and did not intend to lose any more, he could do as he liked. Costler was a carpenter by trade, and knew, he said, he could make more money down there than he could digging, so we told him to go, and we sold Billey for one hundred and fifty dollars, divided up every dollar we had made, and he left us. I never saw him again for two years, when I met him in Nevada City. He told me he had been on the run from one place to another ever since.

After Costler left us, See and I continued to work on Morris' ravine with varied success. The gold was nuggety—some days we would get nothing—then the sinking was some six or seven feet. To strip a "paddock," as it is called (a hole), one would dig down seven or eight feet, and, perhaps, get nothing; then again one might get three or four nuggets running in weight from one to four ounces, and some small or fine gold. In Morris' ravine one depended wholly upon the nuggets he might get. We worked there some time when See got suddenly homesick, and go home he must and did. He would have about one thousand dollars when he got back—that was all he wanted, he said—that would finish up paying for his farm. He had a wife and one child, and he could make a living for them when he had his farm paid for, and he departed. That left me alone, and lonesome enough I was. One night I went over to Long's Bar for some groceries and meat, for there was a regular butcher's shambles. The butcher's name was Jerre Armstrong, from near Morris, Illinois, and he persuaded me to come to the bar and try my luck in a wing-dam. He offered me a half share. I thought it a good offer, so did all that I talked with, and so I came. Board was twenty-one dollars a week, and I went to work on Long's Bar wing-dam. The third day a man came along and hired out for sixteen dollars a day. No· one knew who he was or where he came from. He was carrying over stone with me, with a hand-barrow, and just as he had discharged his load he stepped on a stone that turned, and he fell into the stream. The current was swift and it carried him down until he struck the eddy, when he suddenly turned over, threw up his hands and sank, and that was the last ever seen of him. So it has been with hundreds of men who have gone to California, met with some accident, and, being unknown, their friends could not be written to; they died among strangers and were soon forgotten.

When we had worked about four weeks on the dam, and had got nearly ready to rock the golden dirt, a flood came, as disastrous to our hopes as Noah's was to the ancient world, and swept everything away. I made up my mind that would be the last wing-dam, or any other kind of dam, that I would invest in in California. At that time there was a craze for river damming. There was one just below Long's, and another, the White Rock company's, where the dam and cutting, to turn the river, cost over a hundred thousand dollars that season, and they did not even get into the river. Besides, at every turn or bend in the stream, there was a company wing-damming. In my opinion, there was not one dollar got out of the river where ten dollars were put in. There was a good class of people there—that is, the majority, for there are always exceptions, and Long's Bar was not without its exceptions. On the other side of the river from Long's, lived a Mr. Adams and his wife, from Quincy, Illinois. I shall never forget that lady; she was like a sister to me. I was young, and she knew the temptations that were placed in the way of a boy of my age, thrown in among gamblers, inexperienced, and no one to advise him, so she took it upon herself to do so, and very thankful am I for it. She was the only woman on that side of the river, and I think there were none on the other side. The two Armstrong brothers were engaged in the butchering business. They were like brothers to me for the short time I was there. The following circumstance occurred while I was there:

The Armstrongs used to bring up cattle from the Sacramento flat in droves of a dozen or twenty at a time, and herd them down by a little bend in the river that was perfectly hemmed in by high clifts of rocks, so it was impossible for them to get out except by the way they were brought in. The inclosure embraced about ten acres. One Sunday afternoon Jerre Armstrong took his minie rifle on his shoulder and a pail of salt, and went down to salt his cattle. After about two hours he returned and lay down on his bunk. He looked very pale and I asked him if he was sick. "No," said he, "why do you ask?" I told him that he was as white as a ghost, and he was all of a shake. He said he had been nearly frightened to death. Said he went down to count the cattle and salt them, and then started for home, and as he was walking towards the entrance of the inclosure, he heard something walking behind him. He paid no attention to it, when suddenly he felt a terrible blow on the shoulder, that knocked him forward three or four feet, and a terrible growl. Looking back over his shoulder there was a grizzly bear making for him with mouth wide open. He said he believed he let out one of the most unearthly yells that ever came from a human being, at the same moment giving a backhanded blow with his rifle which struck the bear full in the mouth; then ran to the top of a hill, about ten yards distant, and fell. As he fell he turned to look for the bear, expecting the next instant to be chewed into mincemeat. To his surprise and joy the bear was down on the bottom and making the best of leg-bail in his power. I examined his rifle, and there were the prints and scratches on the barrel where it had come in contact with the grizzly's teeth. It was an exciting theme of talk in the neighborhood for many a day. The grizzly is as great a terror in California as the tiger is in Hindustan.

Rich Bar, on the west branch of the north fork of Feather river, just to the east of where we fell in with the Oregon party, was the location of the prospecting party, before mentioned, that gave us their surplus of provisions. There had been some very rich findings, and many were going there. Armstrong brothers wanted me to go, as one of them was going while the other remained to manage their business. They had plenty of horses, so I agreed to go with Isaiah, the younger of the brothers, and another young fellow, Horace King, from Illinois. We started in company with three more, for it was reported that the Indians were troublesome and it was not safe to go in small parties. Nelson's creek was the first stream to cross. We camped one night in the mountains above the north fork, on a piece of marshy ground, where there were patches of scrub. In the morning our horses were gone. King and I went out in search of them. After a little we separated and took different routes. Not long after, I struck the trail of the horses making down towards the camp. I was crossing over a sandy place, when all at once I heard something "zit" past, close to my head. Soon another "zit." I did not have to think twice to make up my mind what it was. As it is sometimes expressed, I did not run, but I did some pretty tall walking. I did not look back, but before I reached a little rise of ground, or spur of a hill, five of those "zits" had sounded at regular intervals in my ear. As I reached the rise, which was not more than thirty yards, I saw a large bowlder that had rolled down from a higher level. I jumped to the top of it and suddenly turned around just in time to see nothing but a bunch of long grass move a little. I up gun and fired into the centre of the bunch, and left for camp. The boys had heard my shooting, and inquired what I had been shooting at. I told them a bunch of grass. "Did I kill it?" I said I did not go to look. We talked about that bunch of grass until there seemed to be a mysterious fascination in the subject, and all had a desire to inspect it a little closer, so we all went together, taking, of course, our guns with us. Arriving at the spot we were all surprised to find an Indian stretched out at full length, fast asleep, as we supposed, but on closer inspection we found he had a little bullet hole through him, just under his armpits. He was taking his last sleep.

We went on up to Rich Bar and found many digging there. It was all crevicing, that is, working the crevices in the rocks. Some had made an immense pile in a few weeks. I met the party there who had given us the provisions while we were with the Oregon party. They had all done well. There were no claims, but every man started out in the morning with his crowbar, iron spoon

and tin dish, and looked for a crevice to work out. Some
of them had many pounds of gold. One man obtained
as much as a pint cup full in one day, which I had observation of myself. We staid there two or three weeks and
prospected around in different cañons with a little success;
but on the whole it was not a paying trip, and we soon
got tired. Armstrong wanted to go back to Long's Bar
to his butchering business, and the rest of us were quite
willing to. So we departed, stopping on our way back
to prospect on Nelson's creek for a week, but met with
nothing encouraging. We never went out without our
guns or revolvers, as we were liable at any moment to
meet the infernal redskins. One day I was out looking
for the horses and came across some acorns, the largest
I ever saw, and gathered a few as a specimen to show the
boys in camp. As I had them in hand, intently looking at
them, I was wholly oblivious of anyone near me, but as
I raised my eyes to start, I saw two Indians directly facing me, within forty feet, with their bows drawn and the
arrows just ready to fly. Selkirk was inspired by loneli-
ness when he was supposed to have said:

> "How fleet is a glance of the mind!
> Compared with the speed of its flight
> The tempest itself lags behind,
> And the swift winged arrows of light.
> When I think of my own native land,
> In a moment I seem to be there;
> But alas! recollection at hand
> Soon hurries me back to despair."

Never, until that moment, did I appreciate those lines.

I thought of my mother, my home, every act of my childhood; everything I had done in my life up to that moment, flashed across my mind in rapidly successive installments. Instinctively and without reflection, caused by the startling realities of the moment, as I now suppose, I flirted, rather than threw, the acorns in their faces. That act was a surprise to them and caused them to wince, and their arrows, which were sent at the same instant, to miss their mark. Now was my opportunity, and I availed myself of it. Before they could put their hand over their shoulder and draw another arrow from the quiver, I had my revolver, and in an instant there were two more red-skins ready for the tan-yard, but whose hides where too badly damaged to command full price.

Our Nelson creek prospecting proved as unprofitable as our Rich Bar had, so we came to the conclusion to return to Long's Bar again. Shortly after our arrival, being in Adams' store one evening, I met a newly arrived party, one of whom, after eyeing me for a time, asked me if I did not know him? I could not recognize him. He said he was Charlie Young, from Young's mill, Farmington, Ohio. For the moment I was so confused that I could remember nothing, although I knew him well. When my senses came back to me I felt exceeding delight, for he was the first person I had yet seen since I left home whom I had known before. He told me his father and John Proctor, another Farmington boy, were up on Middle Fork, four miles above Burwell's Bar, twelve miles from where we then were, and the next day I went up to see them. Burwell's Bar was on the main Feather river, eight miles above Long's Bar. Two miles above Burwell's the river forked, one branch forming the South, the other the Middle fork of the Feather river. Up the Middle two miles is, or was, Miller's Bar, and here I found Elisha Young and John Proctor, two old Farmington acquaintances from my early childhood. It is needless to say that this meeting, in that far-distant, uncivilized, rocky, craggy region of the Sierra Nevada mountains, was mutually joyous. One who has been there and been fortunate enough to meet one of his early friends or acquaintances can appreciate such a meeting. I say fortunate enough, for it is one of the best events in a young man's life, so situated, who has any pride and self-respect, to meet, occasionally, with early companions, and especially those from home. It has a tendency to keep him steady, for nothing is more dreaded by a young man than to have a report go back to his early friends and childhood home that he has gone to the bad. I have known many that had become reckless and had gone down, brought back by falling in with one of the companions of his youth, when that one was of the right kind; otherwise they both go down, cursing their luck, as all miners choose to call their misfortunes or ill success, when ninety-nine times in a hundred it is their own fault.

Young and Proctor were working on Miller's Bar, washing the sand that had been thrown up among the bowlders, and making good wages. They proposed that I should go to work with them, which I did, but after all they were disinclined to remain there, and were constantly talking of what could be done in Marysville, in the milk business. They wanted to go down there and buy cows and sell milk, and at last they got me equally interested in their scheme. We finally sent Proctor down to see what could be done, and Young and I suspended work till his return having become too thoroughly enthused in the milk project to even dig gold. After a week he returned, and great was the account he gave us of what could be done in milk, in Marysville. Like Colonel Seller's eye-water, there was "millions in it." So off to Marysville, about forty miles distant, we went. As I had some things at Long's Bar, it was arranged for me to go down that way, while they would go the more direct route. But when I got back to Long's Bar, Mr. Adams and his wife, whom I have already mentioned, endeavored to persuade me out of the milk business, offering me two hundred dollars a month to work for them. They were running a store at the Bar, and her brother had a four-horse team on the road, between there and Sacramento. They would put on another team for me to drive. They were so solicitous for my welfare and so generous in their proposals that I partly, or rather conditionally, promised to accept. The brother had that morning started for Sacramento, and was to stop at a ranch a day, and I was to start at once and overtake him. We were to buy the team in Sacramento and I was to drive it back, if, after I had seen Young and Proctor, they would let me off. I overtook the brother, who was also anxious for me to go right on with him, but I felt under obligations of honor to see Young and Proctor first, and, therefore, I went on to Marysville and found them. They had arrived there before me, and I found Young already dissatisfied. He claimed that Proctor's imagination was too brilliant, and his colors too gaudy for a rural picture of cows, cans and milkmaids. The end of the milk business. Young wanted me to return with him to Miller's Bar. While I was now in a quandary as to whether I ought to go back to the Bar with Young or go on to Sacramento in the teaming enterprise, a circumstance occurred that changed all my previous plans, and probably all my after life.

Before I left Farmington, Ohio, a party from that town and vicinity had left for California, among whom were Shurben H. Loveland, Lyman Wolcott, James Holly, Benj. Johnston, John Moore and Daniel Powell, all of whom I had known from my childhood. James Holly was my cousin. I met a man from Nevada City who knew the party and told me some had died; that Holly and Johnston had died and Moore had returned home; that the rest were in Nevada City and he could direct me right to their cabin. That was enough; nothing less than a double-locked prison would have been able to hold me from going at once to the boys.

But before taking the reader to Nevada City, it may be of interest to say something of the Marysville of that day. Those who have known it in later years can judge somewhat of the change which time has wrought between 1850 and 1887. When I first arrived there, it probably contained about twenty-five hundred inhabitants. Nearly all the buildings were frames, covered either with canvas or paling split out of pine, six feet long, and nailed on like clapboards, with generally a rather gaudy looking front, covered with a flashy sign, especially the gambling houses, such as the Montezuma, Eldorado, Magnolia and other similar names. All these houses were equipped with a drinking bar running the entire length of the building, where the frequenters of the house could always procure refreshments for the inner man in the shape of cocktails, sangarees, mint-juleps, sherry-cobblers, in fact, every possible concoction that the mind of man could devise to extract money from the miner when he came down from the mines with his nuggets and bags of dust, and who, in almost every instance, spent his money like a prince, or rather like a fool. At the farthest end of the room one would observe a platform or stage for a band of musicians or singers, the performers varying in number according to the business of the house. In front of the bar and all through the room were tables from four to six feet long; on each side was seated a man, and in the centre was a pile of silver dollars and gold coin, principally doubloons, a Spanish coin equal to sixteen of our dollars. At other tables were roulettes, A B C games, in fact every thing that could induce the miner to spend his money. The early history of gambling in the gold regions of the west is not the most edifying reading; besides, it is too long, and the story and the narrator are often deemed alike incredible. I venture, however, to relate a single instance which fell under my own observation: Two miners came down from Rich's Bar, on Feather river, on their way home to the states, with $14,000 between them, and, stopping at Marysville over night, of course visited one of the gambling houses, made at first some small investments in the "bank," which at first seemed profitable, and soon got warmed up to make larger investments and take greater risks, and the result was, the next morning they found their last dollar gambled away, when they returned to the mines dead broke. I ought perhaps to balance the foregoing instance by relating another a little more cheering, on account of the tender age of one who boldly "bucked the tiger." A butcher there had a little brother about twelve years old, who went into a gambling house one evening with eight dollars, and at midnight he went home with $2,400. The brother took it from him and laid it safely away. The next day the boy was begging of his brother to let him go back and try his luck again, but he would not let him go till evening, when he gave him eight dollars more and let him start out. He returned with $800 more, when his brother took it as before and promised to keep it safe for him and invest it so that he would have it with interest when he should become of age, and then told him if he ever went into a gambling house again to gamble, he would put him aboard the next ship that sailed and send him home. There was but little commercial business done in Marysville, except a little packing for the upper Feather river. Most of the trade went to Sacramento. Towns were springing up like mushrooms. Yuba City was already noted, but for not much more then than for its gambling houses.

One day, while walking through the market of Marysville, I saw some pears for sale. I had seen no fruit yet in the country. All my boyish appetite was aroused. I took one and ate it and was about to take another, when it occurred to me to ask how much they were apiece, at the same time pulling out a silver dollar to pay for the two. It somewhat jogged the intellect when in a modest and innocent way I was told that they were only $2.50 apiece. I suddenly discovered that the one I had already eaten was sufficient for me at that time. I paid for it and walked on to meet a vender of onions, who told me that he was disposing of his vegetables for the remarkably low price of $3 a pound. I purchased of him one good large onion for $2, and ate it raw, and thought I had never before tasted anything half so delicious. Up to this time there had been no fruit imported into the country, except dried apples and peaches, which were to be had at one dollar a pound; dried Chili beans at the same price; pickled peaches at $16 a gallon; jar onions and cucumbers and other like pickles at $8 per half gallon jars. So it is manifest that one had to make something to live; yet scarcely anyone ever stinted himself even at the above prices. Board was $21 a week at the most common boarding-houses. The food was mostly pork and beans, plenty of bread and beef, the latter the cheapest article of food in the country; dried apple sauce, tea and coffee, and all this ample bill of fare for $21 a week, or for $1.50 per meal. Such was the case wherever I went, up to the summer of 1851, when garden vegetables began to be raised plentifully. I remember paying one dollar a pound for potatoes. We could not afford ourselves the luxury of eating them boiled, but used to slice them up like cucumbers, with vinegar. This was not for the love of them in this style, but as a preventive of scurvy.

When potatoes got down to $30 a hundred pounds, my-
self and another bought each a hundred pounds, and
carried them on our backs three miles, thinking we had a
great prize.

CHAPTER X.

Nevada City — Wood's Ravine—Ohio Boys — Miners' Generosity — Gamblers and Gambling — Judge Lynch's Court—Ohio Party Rescued—Rough and Ready—Mrs. Phelps and Her Pies—First Woman in Nevada City — Church Bazaar Post-office — The Scales—First Newspaper—Deference to Woman.

I WAS now determined to see the Ohio boys at Nevada City, as it was then thus early called, about thirty-five miles from Marysville, up in the Sierra Nevada mountains. I struck out one morning as soon as daylight and followed up the Yuba river for some miles, passing through a place called Long Bar. It was more than a mile long. The river was then very low, for the snow had all melted and it was the miners' harvest. I was asked more than twenty times if I wanted to hire out, the wages offered being sixteen dollars a day. But as I had set my heart on finding the boys from my old neighborhood in Farmington, Ohio, sixteen dollars a day had no tempting charms for me. It is utterly impossible for me to describe the feelings of anxiety to see them. I had been a boy always living in a country town, had never been among strangers till leaving home, and had seen none since but strangers; but now that I was about to mingle among my early childhood companions, it seemed to me I could not control my impatience to get to them. But time brings an end to everything, and so it did to my journey from Marysville to Nevada City.

I made Wood's Ravine, on the west side of Nevada City, about four o'clock the same day. My informant had directed me so correctly and minutely that I was enabled to go to their cabin without difficulty or even inquiry. I rapped at the door. O, how my heart beat with anxiety for fear that the man had misinformed me, for somehow I had forebodings that he was mistaken as to the party, and when a stranger came to the door my heart sank in agony. I told him I had made a mistake, I thought. That I had been informed that a party lived there of the name of Loveland, Powell and Wolcott. And now how my heart leaped with joy when I heard a voice from within say, "Yes, Charlie, we are all here, come in." That voice was Lyman Wolcott's. He was sick in bed and the stranger was taking care of him. The other boys were out at work and would all be in at night. It seemed to me like being at home again among my own people. The boys did not get home till dark, and we lit no light until they came, so as to see if they would know me by my voice. Loveland came first; he knew me at once. I thought Powell would not, as I had grown considerably since he had seen me or heard my voice. Soon he came in while I was sitting by Wolcott's bed talking to him, and went directly to wash himself. All at once he stopped and rushed across the cabin to me and exclaimed: "Deacon Ferguson or his ghost! I will swear that is his voice." Unlike the Dutchman who explained that the reason why he called his son

Conrad was because that was his name, the boys of my neighborhood in Ohio called me "deacon" because I had none of the sober and sedate qualities or characteristics of that excellent church official. So neither got the laugh on the other. We were all mutually delighted at this meeting in this part of the world so remote from our native home. My pleasure was greatly enhanced from the fact that I now heard from home, at least indirectly, which I had not since I left Illinois.

Of course I was to stop there. I could, they said, do as well there, if not better, than elsewhere. We would be all together, knew each other, and, what was more, they had heard from home and were expecting a lot of the boys out every day from Ohio. They were coming across the plains and were sure to be there, they said, in a few days. And sure enough it proved true, for in a very short time they got word that the company were coming by the Truckee route, and were then camped some seventy-five to one hundred miles out; that their oxen had given out, and what was worse they were out of provisions. They had sent word by some emigrants who were a little better off and able to proceed, but still had nothing to share. Seldom if ever at that stage of the journey would a party have a surplus. They got the news in the morning, and by two o'clock in the afternoon, Loveland and Powell had bought five mules and started with three packed with provisions to meet the starving and distressed Ohio boys. So it was, universally, throughout California; it only needed to be known that one was in want, and there were always willing hearts and hands, yes, and money too, to

relieve. No matter how total a stranger it might be who
was distressed, the miners rose to every occasion. There
was something about those rough exteriors which enclosed
such great and generous hearts, that makes my very soul
stir within me as I contemplate them now, when time
and death and distance have separated us forever. They
had all suffered and knew what it was to suffer, and when
they heard of one in distress, their time, their money was
nothing—their only thought was concerning the most
speedy and effective relief.

Many are the gamblers even, whom I have seen, on hearing of some poor fellow who was sick or in want, put his
hand in his pocket and pull out twenty or thirty dollars
and hand it over, saying nothing more than, "Give that
to him," and try at the same time to look unconcerned
or indifferent; but scanning his countenance closely, one
would see his lips quiver and his eye gathering moisture
as he listened to the sorrowful tale. I venture to say right
here that if I were sick, without money, without acquaintance, and among strangers, if honest and deserving, I
would rather fall among those rough California or Australian miners, and gamblers even, than among many
eastern men of wealth whom I know, who make broad
their phylacteries and assume the virtues that should come
of Christian civilization. The latter would refer me to the
relief committee who would send me

"Over the hills to the poor-house;"

while the former would put his hand in his pocket and
hand out immediate relief, or take me by the hand and say,
"Come along, Cap, you can turn into my hut until some-

thing turns up; I think I know of something for you when you are well enough; in the meantime, stop with me and we will see what can be done. If you are sick, bring a doctor. Say to him that you have no money. He will say, 'never mind, we will talk of the pay when you get well.'" That was the sort of stuff the early pioneers of California were made up of, and thousands will bear me out in this statement. Those were trying times, and they tried the qualities of men; and the nobler instincts of man became there a law unto themselves, even like unto the golden rule to do unto others as you would like to be done by. Had it got abroad that one had refused to relieve a fellow in want, he would have been lynched sooner than for stealing a mule, and heaven knows that that was not only abundantly speedy, but sure as death or taxes. However, with the exception of cases of sickness, there was less want in California, even at that time, than in any country I was ever in

I abhor gambling in all places and in all forms, whether it be in mining regions or Wall street, or whether it be done at wholesale or retail. But society considers and treats gambling very much as it does the liquor traffic. It prosecutes and punishes the retailer and sends the distiller and brewer to the legislature and to congress. It legislates against betting on elections and horse racing as a bad and disgraceful business. But betting becomes respectable and legitimate when made on the price of wheat in Chicago, or railroad and mining stocks in New York, and the man who can "corner" the wheat market or bring to ruin the original stockholders, whose honest

money built the road, is a hero, and such wholesale gamblers are called "kings." When the hypocrite, who has
been regarded by confiding women and children as a
saint, takes up his permanent residence in Canada, with the
funds of a savings bank, he is never spoken of as a thief or
robber, but always respectfully referred to as a financier.
When a railroad official converts to his own use, or "mis-
appropriates," as the financial term is, a million dollars,
his colleagues may growl a little, but when he endows a
theological seminary, or consecrates a memorial window
to the relict of the deacon of his church, society is compla-
cent and rejoices in the apparent belief that, after all, his
virtues balanced his rascalities.

When we came into California the territory had only
just been annexed to the United States. Immigration
soon commenced to pour in rapidly, and as there were no
law-makers, consequently there was no law—at least we
were told so by the rough element, which is always a
numerous class when a sudden influx of people are thrown
together under great excitement, such as was produced by
the gold-fever, and that class will find one another out
quicker than any other; but the better class are always
sure to rule in the long run, and so it was in California.
The thieves and robbers boasted that we had no law, but
were told that laws could soon be made for them and all
such as were not disposed to be law-abiding. And so
there was, for as soon as there was a case of theft or robbery, the culprit was hunted down. We would sometimes
hear of men running around, with rope in hand, crying
out for the hanging of a thief or robber, under such a state

NEVADA CITY, 1851.

of excitement that possibly an innocent man might suffer, but generally cooler men would come to the front, and never in all my experience did I either know or hear of an excited crowd carrying their designs into execution until the culprit had had a fair and impartial trial, according to the forms prescribed in the unwritten code of Lynch law. The proceedings of Judge Lynch's court, which I have attended, were something like this: The culprit being secured, the crowd would adjourn to some proper place, when they would elect a judge, who would be generally the most prominent and influential man of the town or place, then a jury of twelve men, or sometimes a less number, of like character of the judge, as nearly as possible, as could be found in the place, also a prosecutor, a lawyer, if possible, also, if the party accused had no friends, they would appoint the most competent man to be found for his lawyer. The tribunal being thus constituted, witnesses were examined and arguments made by the counsel, perhaps, when the jury would bring in their verdict of guilty or not guilty, and if guilty the judge passed sentence. If for stealing, the sentence was for a certain number of lashes, more or less, according to the enormity of the crime and the previous character of the culprit. Such was the invariable course pursued, except when the criminal was caught in the act, when no trial was deemed necessary. I never witnessed but one lynching by hanging, and that was an Indian. I shall hereafter have occasion to allude to the subject of Lynch law.

Loveland and Powell found the boys they started out to relieve, on the third or fourth day. The party consisted of Henry G. Taft, Homer Stull, brother of Judge John M. Stull of Warren, Trumbull county, Ohio; Ira and Amaziah Ross and Samuel Strickland, all from my old town of Farmington, in that county. There were also in the company Austin Perry from Mesopotamia, same county; a Mr. Mayhew of Bristol, Trumbull county; Samuel Beecher, of Mantua; George Raymond of Hiram, Portage county; and another man from the latter place whose name I cannot recall, but who, poor fellow, was accidentally shot by one of the party, just as Loveland and Powell found them. And so it was that, after all his toil and sufferings for want of food, he was killed almost the same moment that relief arrived. So the camp was in a state of mourning when otherwise it would have been a scene of rejoicing. They buried him as Sir John Moore was buried—

"No useless coffin enclosed his breast."

Their teams having got somewhat rested, they started back for Nevada, arriving in due time, and there was great rejoicing on both sides, they that their long and toilsome journey was ended, we to see them and to hear from our dear old home and the loving ones we had left behind. No one knows how dear home and friends are unless one has been separated from them. I know from sad experience. I shall have occasion hereafter to allude to many of the above names. Many of them are now dead. Some died before I left California, particularly George Raymond, Horgan, and Austin Perry, whom I had known for many years. Homer Stull lived to return, but afterwards died defending our flag and Union; but his memory still lives, associated with his generous spirit. Henry G. Taft, a specimen of God's noblest work, still lives and is in South America, as I have recently (1887) learned from his brother in Warren, Trumbull county, Ohio.

Nevada City, it should be borne in mind, is not a town in the state of Nevada, but is in California among the Sierra Nevada mountains, on the western slope, situated on Deer creek, eight miles south of the south fork of the Yuba river, and about four miles northeast of Grass valley, so called by those who first came to Nevada City taking their cattle there to pasture, there being no grass near the town. Gold had not yet been discovered in Grass valley. About half way between the two places was what was afterwards called Gold Run, that eventually proved to be very rich, and which I shall have occasion to allude to hereafter. Down Deer creek about four miles was Boyer's Agency. He was supposed to be some kind of an Indian agent, although I was never able to learn what he did for the Indians or any one else but himself. This remark is not intended in disparagement of Mr. Boyer, but only that I can't see what the government or the Indians wanted of an agent there. About half way between Boyer's and Nevada City was Wood's Ravine, so named after a man of that name who lived there and afterwards officiated as alcalda or magistrate. About nine miles down Deer creek was Rough and Ready diggings, named, I suppose, from the political campaign title bestowed on President Taylor; but this place was even less complimentary to the President than was suggested by the name, for a harder and more dismal place I never saw.

Nevada City was laid out in a deep ravine. It had its Main street and its Broad street and its Kiota street parallel with Main and a few cross streets. What buildings were erected in my time were on Main and Broad principally. On the south side of Deer creek was the road to Sacramento and towns below, and here Bowers Brothers had their express office. They took letters to San Francisco for the modest sum of two dollars and fifty cents each. I have paid them ten dollars at a time for letters. One Baxter, who had been clerking for them, finally started into the same business himself, having his office on Broad street. There was one business house in Nevada City, attractive to all, and which was eminently successful from the hour of opening its front door. It was Mrs. Phelps' pie house. Mrs. Phelps had a husband; nevertheless, she was the man of the house. They had crossed the plains and brought a cooking stove. Upon arriving at Nevada City, Mrs. Phelps commenced making dried apple pies, which sold readily at one dollar a pie, and coffee at ten cents a cup. She drove a wonderful trade, especially on Sundays when the miners came to town, they having played euchre every evening of the week to determine who should pay for the pies when they went to the "city." She often found it impossible to supply the demand on that day, notwithstanding her efforts in anticipation of increased numbers. She soon increased her facilities for business by getting another stove and purchasing a couple of bright-looking cows, which made her place look home-like and were a great attraction. There was such a demand for milk that it readily sold at a dollar a pint, and one-half water at that. I have often seen her place literally thronged with miners waiting for her pies to come out of the oven, and as soon out, devoured. I think she was the first woman that arrived in Nevada City. Mrs. Coates, who came across the plains, was the second; Miss Bowers, sister of the Bowers brothers, was the third; a Mrs. Scott, who settled out on Rock creek, was the fourth; and Mrs. George Scott was the fifth. These women were a great attraction, and had they put themselves up on exhibition they would have drawn great houses. But they were brave, noble and virtuous women. They were not only anxious to make money by honest industry, but also to improve society, and they had not been long among us before their presence and cheering influence were felt in more ways than one. They put shoulder to the wheel, and soon a church was under way. They were angels of mercy, and many a poor suffering soul received assistance, comfort and consolation from their motherly and sisterly hands and gentle spirits. They were loved and respected by everyone in and around Nevada City.

The first storekeepers, as I now remember, were Davis & Hurst, on the corner of Broad and a street that ran across to Kiota street. The first principal bakers and butchers were Napper & Webster. Of professional men Dr. Gardner was considered the chief. He died early in 1851, lamented by all. Dr. Livermore was a dentist who came there from Sidney, Australia. Time has obliterated the memory of many names with which I was then and there familiar, but I recall a noble-hearted southern gentleman, Dr. Weaver, from Memphis, Tennessee. He owned the place called White Hall, at the head of Broad street, which will be remembered by many as the place where the ladies held their first bazaar, for the building of the first church. I remember it distinctly, and I pity the poor fellows that were beset by the ladies as I was. Miss Bowers kept the "post-office" at that bazaar, and no sooner than a fellow got inside, after paying two dollars entrance fee, than he was notified by the pleasant post-mistress that there was a letter in the office for him. I was young and felt quite flattered when notified by that young lady, in her most winsome manner, that she had in her official keeping a letter for me. I stepped up and received a letter at her hands, and was in the act of returning her gracious smile, as best fitted my countenance, when she said, in the sweetest of womanly accents, "Two dollars and fifty cents." I paid it with alacrity. When I opened it I found it to be written in Dutch or Indian, not a word of which could I make out. I was not wise enough to keep the joke to myself, but must go and tell her. "Dear me, how stupid I was," said she; "but here is your letter," handing me another. I was innocent enough to receive it, when the same sweet seductive voice repeated: "Two dollars and a half," and I again discharged my obligation to the post-office without shedding a tear. Mrs. Phelps ran the pie and coffee stand, and succeeded admirably in her line. I was not long in falling in with Mrs. Scott, who kept the scales. "Dear me," said that lady, "is that you? Why I hardly knew you. Have you been sick?" I innocently said, "No." "How I had fallen away!" I thought not, but she was sure I had.

"Just step on the scales and she would see." I did not drop to her little game, but like a simpleton mounted the scales as she requested, and weighed five pounds more than usual. "Well, well, I was mistaken," but smiling, she said: "People are liable to be deceived. Two dollars, please." I paid it and walked away, fully agreeing with Mrs. Scott that people are liable to be deceived, particularly at a ladies' church bazaar. I had not been in the house more than an hour when my experience had cost me about thirty dollars. I don't remember how much the fair netted, but it was something enormous. The miners were captivated with the smiles of the ladies and were willing to pay liberal for one; nor were the ladies sparing of their blandishments, so long as the miners' money held out. The gamblers, too, came in for their share, and got as handsomely fleeced as they ever fleeced a poor miner.

Hubbard & Hodge was the first law firm I remember. They had all they could do to prevent litigation and keep peace among the people. Main street contained three large gambling houses, fitted up in the most elaborate style—Barker's, Antonio's and George Scott's. Broad street had only two, the Central and White Hall. There were, however, an endless number of small concerns that we cannot record, both in and around Nevada. Over the hill, near Lessen's tunnel, lived a character who may still be remembered by some of the present residents—the Dutch blacksmith, politician and stump orator. There were others I may have occasion to mention hereafter.

Early in 1851 the government granted Nevada City a post-office. It was a blessing to all, for we could now write to our friends at home and send and receive letters direct, without the expense of two dollars and a half express charges between there and San Francisco. I have forgotten the postmaster's name. About the same time the first newspaper made its appearance, displaying in good clear letters its title, *Nevada Chronicle*. I am also at fault, at this late day, as to the name of the editor, but have been told that the enterprising gentleman became a man of note in the state, and was appointed minister to Prussia and afterwards to Russia. Davis and Hurst built the first theatre in Nevada City, or in the Sierra Nevada mountains. The first company that appeared on its boards was under the management of Dr. Robinson. Many will remember the gentleman by his celebrated Yankee stories, told in the name of Hesekiah Pickerell. The first play I witnessed was "Christopher Strap." Soon, however, they aspired to something higher, as society was rapidly becoming more cultivated and select, and the "Lady of Lyons" was placed upon the boards, Mrs. Robinson taking the rôle of the lady, and a young man named Edwards that of Claude Melnotte. Bowling alleys and billiards were not long in coming in, so that by the latter part of '51 Nevada City society was not without abundant places and varieties of amusement. A store was established in Wood's Ravine by a man from Arkansas, whose last name was James. The summer of '51 is especially remembered from the circumstance of the death of his wife. The community deeply sympathized with him, but, moreover, each person seemed to mourn as for a personal affliction and inconsolable loss, such was the regard and reverence for woman where there were so few. When the death of a woman was announced in a distant mining camp, a sudden sadness and silence pervaded; men spoke low to each other, and the cabin door was opened and closed lightly, as if for fear of disturbing the dead. James subsequently entered into a business partnership with Mrs. Coates, whom I have before mentioned. They started a boarding-house in connection with the store, and drove a flourishing business. Mrs. Coates was a very cheerful woman, and her kind and pleasant disposition made her house very attractive, and her vivacious spirit was a stimulating medicine to my own and many other miner's dreary and lonesome life. I have sometimes feared that an erroneous notion prevailed in the states that the pioneer women of the early California times were of a low order, and were regarded by the delvers in the mountains and looked upon by them as base adventurers of an immoral character; but such has not been my experience. I never knew a miner to insult a woman, but, on the other hand, I know a woman could visit alone a camp of miners and be treated with higher consideration than many honorable wives, mothers and sisters are treated by men in passing along the streets of our cities in the evening, or even in the day-time. Every miner seemed to consider himself her sworn guardian, policeman and protector, and the slightest dishonorable word, action or look of any miner or other person, would have been met with a rebuke he would remember so long as he lived, if,

perchance, he survived the chastisement.   No matter how
"rich and rare were the gems she wore,"

> "But blest forever was she who relied
> Upon a miner's honor and a miner's pride!"

CHAPTER XI.

Mining Associations—A Claim—Rifle Bounded—Kiote Diggings—
Hiring Out—"Galena"—Senator Stewart—Painful Sickness—
Poor Man's Creek — Borrowing a Mule — Another Grizzly
— Perry's Death—Ingratitude—Jumping a Claim—First Min-
ing Suit—Eviction—The Evictor Evicted—Luck—A Miner's
Superstition.

HAVING digressed in the last chapter to make brief
mention of Nevada City and its first pioneers, and
while I shall hereafter have occasion to refer to others of
them, I must now return to the time of my arrival at the
Ohio boys' hut.　In the company that Loveland and
Powell went out to relieve and bring in, were two other
persons whose names I omitted—William Powell, brother,
and Edward McCall from Parkman, Geauga county,
Ohio.　The rescued company all camped with us until they
could build a hut.　Taft, Stull, Mayhew, Strickland and
the two Rose brothers were under a home contract of
partnership to share alike, so they went in together.
Many in that early day came out under like arrangements, but those incipient, home-partnerships never held
long, and were often dissolved before they arrived, certainly within three months after reaching their destina-
tion; not always that ill-feeling existed, but the thought

of being bound together was generally sufficient cause for dissatisfaction. So it was in their case, for after remaining together about three months Taft and Strickland drew out, while the other four remained together during their stay in the mountains. William Powell, Beecher, McCall and Raymond built another hut near by, and thus our village of three huts, built on rather elevated ground, got the name of Buckeye Hill. There was a man in the party that came across the plains with Loveland by the name of Fisk, from Nelson, Portage county, Ohio, whose brother had just arrived by way of Panama—had contracted the fever. He had been staying with his brother some three months, unable to work in the mines; so Fisk concluded to sell out his interest in the hut, take his brother down to Sacramento and start gardening. With the approval of the others, I bought him out, including his cooking utensils, for two ounces of gold. Wolcott was about to leave for home, and Taft bought him out at the same price, so that now our party proper consisted of Loveland, Powell, Taft and myself, and we remained together as long as we were in California. Although some one or more were at times away, that was invariably our headquarters and home.

When the mines in and around Nevada City were first opened, they were solely in the ravines. Deer creek was rockbound, and there was no law regulating the size of a miner's claim, and generally a party that first went into a ravine had the exclusive right thereto, or as much of it as he or they saw fit to claim. As population increased that rule did not long maintain. The primitive manner of asserting a claim and the limits thereof, is best illustrated by the following story: An old prospector and miner of the hard-shell type used to take his rifle with him, and when at work set it up against a tree. One day a new-comer arrived in the ravine and asked the old miner some questions, but the answers were all evasive; but when he inquired how much of the ravine he claimed, the old fellow started up bright and communicative, and, pointing to the tree where his rifle leaned, said. "D'ye see that rifle there, stranger?" "Yes," said the man. "Wall," said the miner, "jist as fur as that rifle carries, up and down this ravine, I claim—and no further; there, now, you know." Then he went on about his work. The man left, concluding he would look for diggings elsewhere.

This state of things continued, however, only for a short time. The miners saw that something must be done, and therefore a meeting was called and a rule was established that each miner could hold thirty feet square as a mining claim, but was entitled to buy out as many claims as he pleased, providing he kept men at work on them; and that law held good while I remained in California. When mines were first opened, but few, comparatively, had any knowledge of mining gold, and everyone had a theory of his own. The general impression was that gold lay in the gravel on the bed-rock, and so it did upon granite, and even where the granite was soft it worked itself into that a few inches. Many of the crevices in the ravines near Nevada were slate bed-rock and loose on the edges, and the first workers only took off the gravel, never digging up the slate. I remember Powell telling me of a man who came along when they were at work in Wood's ravine and laughing, said: "What do you think those fellows are doing up there (on the claim above)? Why," said he, "they are digging up the rock for a foot or more down," and all joined him in the laugh except Loveland, who said nothing; but at dinner time he went up to see what they were doing, and as they also had gone to dinner, he dug up two dishes full of the rock and washed it, and in about half an hour came back to the hut with the gold he had obtained, and it was found that there was more gold in the rock than in the gravel. Thus they had to live and learn. It was for a time believed that gold was confined to the ravines and gulleys, and that Nevada diggings would soon be a thing of the past.

Two miners, Heath and Hale, working the gully that ran through the town, or where the town afterwards came to be, came onto a bed of gravel which seemed to run from the gully into a hill, and as they prospected, favorable indications increased. They followed it into the hill and it grew richer and richer as they advanced, and when they got in too far to strip the surface, they had to tunnel and timber, or kiote, as they then called it. From this system the Kiote diggings derived its name. All the hills northwest of Nevada City proved to be very rich, and gave employment to thousands for many years after. The Kiote diggings were in full blast when I arrived there, and there I did my first work. The boys thought I had better hire out until I got a little insight into the business and understood the working of the ground; so I went with them the first day and saw how they worked and timbered up under ground, for it was all under ground, at a depth of from thirty-five to forty-five feet. I took particular notice of the manner of timbering, and in one day found I could do it as well as any of them. The next morning I started out to look for a job. Generally the first question asked me was, "Where did you come from?" I truthfully answered, "Ohio." No, they did not want me. So I traveled that day to the tune played by the same question and answer, till I began to think there was some prejudice against Ohio men. I went home rather crestfallen, and when I told the boys of my day's experience, they laughed, and then told me that Galena lead miners were all the rage there. That gave me my cue, and the next morning I was on the wing bright and early, and had just got into the busy region when I saw some men standing around a shaft, apparently consulting. I stepped up and asked if they wanted to hire any hands. They looked at me, and then came the same old question, "Where are you from?" "From Galena," I replied, which was again the truth, for I was a long way from it. "You are just the man we want," said one of them. They said they had some men working for them that did not understand mining—that they were about to lose their shaft, and asked me to get onto the rope and go down and take a look at it and see if I thought it could be repaired. I lit a candle, got on to the rope, and they lowered me down. I felt rather skittish, but my reputation was at stake, and it would not do to back out now that I had set myself up for a Galena miner. On inspection I found the shaft badly out of order and so pronounced it when I appeared on the surface, but assured

them that I could make it perfectly safe. One remarked
that he supposed I would want a helper. Now what a
helper was I did not know, but thought I would know
when I saw one. So I said of course I could not get along
without a helper, wondering all the while what kind of a
tool a helper was. I felt relieved, however, when one of
them called to a man passing and asked him if he wanted
a job. "That," said the man, "is just what I am looking
for." He was engaged, and I was still more pleased when I
found he had just come across the plains and I was not
liable to be exposed by him in my pretense of being a bona
fide Galena miner. Then came the question as to how much
I would charge. I looked at the sun and remarked that
as it was now about nine o'clock, I would work that day
for twelve dollars, but that if I worked on I should want
sixteen dollars a day. They told me to go ahead, and
down my helper and I went. I set my helper to clearing
out the dirt and rocks that had fallen down around the
shaft, while I took my measures and went to the surface
to fit my timbers. I felt safer above than down in the
shaft. If the whole thing should fall, or the earth cave in,
only the helper would be killed and not the expert Galena
miner. Human nature is selfish to the last, even in the
best regulated families, and I confess to the common infir-
mity. I got my timbers all cut by the time my helper got
the shaft cleared out. Then I and my timbers went down
and we fitted in the first set and made a good job of it,
when I went home. The boys wanted to know how I got
on, and I told them the whole story, and we had a good

laugh over it, and from that time I went by the name of the Galena miner.

The next day I went back. The helper proved to be a good hand, having worked in the coal mines of Pennsylvania, and knew more about such work than I did. It is an old saying that the devil's children have the father's luck. So it was in our case, for we worked on three days, and a better job was never done. When all was in order they were well pleased and offered me the management of the work, the claim being owned by parties that did not themselves work at mining. I remained with them three weeks, when it was found that the claim was not paying. I should have been surprised if it had. However, as I had been paid every Saturday, I was content and lost no sleep. My next employment was by the company of which Loveland and Powell were part owners. Rigby and Peck, two men from Oberlin, Ohio, had originally taken up the claim and sold out to Loveland, Powell and William M. Stewart, since United States senator for the state of Nevada. He came from Mesopotamia, only five miles from my home, and to whom I shall have occasion to allude hereafter I worked for them three weeks, when the water broke in and drowned out all the claims. Mining was suspended for three months. In the meantime I bought out Powell's share, and he afterwards bought out Stewart. We sold a large pile of wash dirt to Herbert Bowers, one of the Bowers brothers. He failed and we lost our money. That's the way the world wagged then and there.

For a long time I had been feeling that something was wrong with me. I had never felt so before—sluggish, tired,

lazy—the latter I had never been guilty of before. Finally
my gums got sore and began to bleed, and I became subject to excruciating pains. The boys sent for Dr. Gardner,
who pronounced it scurvy, contracted in crossing the
plains, induced by exposure, anxiety of mind and starvation He prescribed spruce boughs boiled to a strong
tea, which I was to drink, and nothing else. A wash of
the same with vinegar and tinctured with cayenne pepper,
including a steam bath of the same, at a pretty high
pressure, were the doctor's directions to the boys for my
daily treatment. It was pretty tough treatment, harder
to bear than any I had ever inflicted during my professional
career among my Oregon patients. I was put through
the steam kettle process by the boys for ten days; was
helpless as an infant, having to be carried to and from
my bed. The painful part of my affliction seemed to be in
my feet and legs. The only way for a long time I could
get at ease was in lying on my back on the floor and putting my feet on the table, a luxury I dearly paid for afterwards, for when I came to put them on a level with my
body, the pain was still more unbearable. I would pity
the meanest dog in the world that had the scurvy. But
thanks to Dr. Gardner, the boys, the steam kettle and
raw potatoes sliced in vinegar, after some two weeks my
pains left me, and "Richard was himself again," though
rather thin and scanty, for I could put my finger on the
calf of my leg or on any fleshy part of my body and
press it to the bone, and the indentation would remain
for half an hour, and when the flesh or skin resumed its
smoothness again, a black spot would mark the place of

the pressure. If my readers think the above description of "scurvy treatment" unnecessary, my apology is that it is for their benefit; should they ever get a little mangy and unable to get a doctor, they can avail themselves of the prescription in my case. As I have lived to tell the story I venture to pronounce the above remedy, in the language of learned Sierra Nevada doctors, a "never failing antiscorbutic."

Although I now called myself well, yet I felt I was not the same person I was before. Powell and myself concluded to go up to a place called Poor Man's Creek, having been offered a chance there by some parties who had come down for provisions. They had a good warm hut already built, so we bought a share in their provisions and tools and started up in a few days. The Creek was about thirty miles from Nevada, on the north side of the south fork of Yuba river. I had overrated my strength, and found I could not work. In fact, I gave out before we got to the Creek and what to do we did not know, but seeing a mule that had strayed away from someone I said, "If I could catch that mule I would ride him," although I knew that if caught it would be a case for hanging. Powell said he could catch him, and he did. We made a bridle of the ropes we had around our blankets, put the blankets across his back, and Powell lifting me on we proceeded, keeping a sharp lookout for the owner of the mule. Soon Powell got tired out and he got on behind me, I telling him that if we were to be hung for the mule we might as well get all we could out of him. He was a large, strong animal and carried us both splendidly. At night, after our arrival, we fed him a large loaf of bread and Powell took him to a place where there was good feed and started him on the back track, and that was the last we ever saw or heard of the mule. It was a good thing we started the mule back that night, for it began to snow, and I never saw snow fall as it does in the Sierra Nevada mountains. It was soon fully four feet deep on a level, and we were snowed in tight and fast. We had nothing to do, as we could not get out to our claim to work. We read all the books we had, told all the stories we had ever heard and all we could invent.

One day the monotony of the hut was broken by one of the boys, when he came running in, his eyes extending from their sockets, saying, "Boys, boys, I've seen a grizzly bear! a monster!" We hardly believed him at first, but when he persisted so earnestly in the truth of his statement, we concluded there was something in it; so I went out but did not see the bear, but did see his unmistakable path in the snow. I went in and loaded up our guns and pistols and we started in pursuit. The snow was so deep we could only wallow through and that only by keeping in the great furrow plowed by the bear. We followed for some time, but could get no nearer, apparently, than when we first started, and it is my impression that there was not a man among us that wanted to get any nearer the mighty beast than we were already. I confess I did not, and I was not the biggest coward in the party either. We had followed the bear nearly an hour when we gave up the chase and returned. One of the boys attempted to discharge his gun but found he could not. Then we tried

every gun and pistol, and found to our surprise that not
one would "go off." The secret was that we had wallowed through the snow until the caps had become wet,
and we congratulated ourselves that we had not overtaken
Mr. Grizzly.

We had now been snowed in some four weeks, and it became more and more tedious hibernating in that lonely
place, so Powell and myself thought to get out in the world
once more, and made a break for Nevada. Following the
creek about eight miles, we reached the Yuba river. This
route was much longer than the one by which we came,
but we thought we would get out of the snow sooner by
this way; besides, there would be a hut at the mouth of
the creek where we could stay over night. Having started
early in the morning, we wallowed on eight miles, reaching
Moore and Peck's hut at dark. They were from Mesopotamia, Ohio. Austin Perry, to whom I have before
alluded, had been with them for a time and was out of
health, had had a job of clerking for the Jameses, but was
unable to stand even this kind of labor, and on inquiring about him at Moore and Peck's, we were pained to
learn that he had died the Sunday previous. We were told
that his last request was for a drink of water; that after
breakfast, one went to ask him if he would have a cup of
coffee, but was surprised to find that poor Austin Perry
was no more. He was a young man, well liked by all who
knew him. He always had a pleasant word for everyone,
and he deserved a better fate.

We reached Nevada at noon the next day, having made
twenty-five miles in half the time it had taken us to make

eight the day before. We now found that Homer Stull, Mayhew and the two Roses were about starting for home. The next day after we had left Nevada, they struck, in a dry gulch near their hut, very rich diggings, but they never told one of their acquaintances who had spent time and money to take them provisions and rescue them from starvation a hundred miles away in the wilderness, but let in strangers after they had made their pile. They sold their claim to one of the Perrys for a mere song, who took out more than twice as much after them. The world seems to wag strangely sometimes—rescue a man from death, nurse him and feed him, and ten chances to one he will never requite the favor, but if he has one to bestow, the stranger is the recipient. We found also that Peck and Rigby had jumped our flooded claims. They were the men we bought of, and we were not at all surprised, as we had no reason to expect otherwise, for we knew they were scoundrels, at least Rigby was, and Peck was a fool, which is worse, for I had rather deal with a rogue than with a fool. But Powell and I were not to be bluffed out of our claim. I went to see Rigby, but he would do nothing but sell to us, so we got our tools and went to sinking a shaft. Rigby came out and made a great bluster, but we were not to be bounced by word of mouth, so he went back, and the next day we were served with legal process; but we kept right on until the day of trial, having finished the shaft the same day. Our lawyer made the point that one partner could not jump a claim against his co-partner, but the court overruled him and we were beaten. That was the first mining suit in Nevada. As we had finished the shaft a little before the trial, which was on a Saturday, we had taken out considerable wash dirt, which is the paying dirt sought for in such diggings, and, therefore, early Sunday morning Powell and I got up and set our long tom, as it was called, and commenced to wash the dirt we had taken out. Rigby heard us and started for the sheriff, told what we were doing and demanded that he should be put in immediate possession, but cautioned the sheriff to be careful, as we were desperate men. Soon the sheriff was on the ground with his posse, and came to me where I was washing. I undertook to argue with him to gain time, while Powell went down to see our lawyers, Hubbard and Hodge. But Rigby got impatient and ordered the sheriff to do his duty, so he asked me to remove our tools, and called his posse to help me. They took the long tom, after shutting off the water, and carried it off the claim. As the water ran off, I saw the yellow gold glittering in the box. I seized hold of it and carried it off bodily about fifty yards farther, although at any ordinary time it would have taken two men to do it, but the sight that I had seen gave me for the moment superhuman strength—the gold was so thick in the wet mass in the box that it looked like yellow pudding. I emptied the richest into a tin dish and sunk it in a pool of water, then cleaned out the riffle bar and put the contents into another dish, and commenced to pan it out carefully. Rigby came around, as I knew he would, to have a look at it. I was very civil to him and washed the little I had left in the box down carefully and showed him the contents of the dish, remarking that the whole thing was not worth quarreling about. He expressed his disappointment and said he thought it was better, or he would not have stood out about it. So I knew he did not mistrust that I was deceiving him. After he had gone Powell came, and we washed out what I had hid away, and it turned out greatly beyond our expectations. There was over two hundred dollars worth of pure gold in what we had already washed out, and as much more dirt on top, at the mouth of the shaft, to be washed by somebody. How to buy the claim of Rigby was now the question, for if we went to him, he would drop on our game, as the expression was. The people around were all in our favor, for they considered he had acted a mean part in jumping his partners, and were glad when it turned out so poorly, as they supposed it had. Sam Beecher had chafed Rigby and Peck about it, and asked them what they would take for the claim—we had sent him for that very purpose. They would take, they said, $125.00. We told him to offer one hundred dollars, giving him that amount in the very gold we had taken out to pay for it. The offer was made and accepted, the gold weighed out and in Rigby's purse, but when he came to make the bill of sale, he was thunderstruck when told to make it out to Powell and Ferguson.

We washed out the next day from the remainder of the dirt over two hundred dollars worth more, and then sold the claim to a party from New Zealand for four hundred dollars. So in the long run we came out ahead of Rigby, and the party we sold to did well. They also bought two or three other claims of Powell and myself, claiming that they had better luck in buying of us than of anyone else.

Miners are always superstitious about luck. No matter how it goes with them, everything is attributed to luck, and a philosopher would sometimes almost think some men were guided by some unseen influence or power, for I have known men for years who, no matter what enterprise they enlisted in, were sure to triumph; and then, possibly, luck would forsake them and leave them in poverty, where the fickle goddess of fortune first found them. Nevertheless, you can't make an old miner believe but that there is something in luck.

CHAPTER XII.

GOLD RUN—SHAFT SINKING—TIMBERING—WASH DIRT—THE ENTERPRISE
COMPANY—KIOTE HILLS TUNNELING—GRASS VALLEY—A MIDNIGHT
CRY—QUARTZ MINING—MORTAR AND PESTLE—FIRST STAMP MILLS—
MARK TWAIN'S EXPERIENCE—JOB'S PATIENCE—MRS. COATES—TEAM-
ING TO SACRAMENTO—LOST AND FOUND—NO THANKS—WHERE'S MY
COAT?—CHIEF COOK—NEVADA IN FLAMES—DOCTORS' DUEL—CRIMES
AND PUNISHMENTS—DUELING—BULL-FIGHTING—WOMEN AND IMPROVED
SOCIETY—INDIAN DANCES AND FUNERAL FASHIONS.

AFTER selling out our Nevada claims to the New
Zealanders, Powell and I went over to Gold Run,
about half way between Nevada City and Grass Valley,
where there had been a late rush. These grounds had
been worked a little about the time of the first opening of
the Nevada City mines, but the diggings were wet at that
time, and the miners did not understand how to contend
with the water as they did eighteen months later, nor did
they know anything about driving, or kioting, as it was
then called; and the whole territory being a marsh, it had
to be boxed, that is, solid timbered. The process was to
sink a shaft to the bed-rock, timbering up as they went
down, with slabs, split from pine logs, varying in width
from six to ten inches, and at least two inches thick.
After reaching bed-rock, a well-hole had to be sunk in the

rock to receive the drainage of the shaft, large enough to allow a bucket to fill itself in bailing out the water. This being accomplished, they commenced to open a horizontal drive on the face of the rock, timbering as they proceeded, by putting down a sill, with notches in the ends the thickness of the posts, with a cap piece about three inches shorter than the sill, so as to allow a little slant to the posts, which increased their firmness. If timbers are thus placed and well fitted, they may possibly be crushed, but otherwise will never give way. The crib being made ready for opening the drive, take out the bottom slabs of the shaft, on the side of the intended drive, to the height of from four to six feet, and as the dirt in the drive is removed, put in the second set of timbers, lathing the top with heavy, stout slabs, and the sides, also, if necessary; this is called box-driving. In some very soft or sandy ground another set of timbers, which miners call preventive or temporary, are required for every two feet advance, and as they are put in the lath timbers are driven along from the last set over the preventive set; then remove the dirt for two feet more, and repeat the process, following up with the main timbers. At Gold Run the nature of the ground was such that it had to be solid timbered.

Some old California miner, who may possibly read this page, will not unlikely say: "What is the use of telling us about mining shafts and drivers and sluices? Don't we know all about it?" Yes, very true, and I am not unmindful of the folly of carrying coals to Newcastle, but am conscious, nevertheless, of a new generation who do

not know the process of primitive gold-mining in California, nor of the hard and toilsome labor of him who delved
for gold in '49. The hard realities of the miner's life
divest the golden age of nearly forty years ago of much
of its poetry and romance.

Powell and myself both hired out to one company to
work exclusively underground, timbering in a drive.
Each had a helper to wheel away the dirt to the shaft,
bring the timber and assist in placing it. Their labor was
by far the hardest, yet they received three dollars a day
less than we. The whole ground was one moving bog
from the surface to the wash dirt, which was about one
foot thick, and the width of paying dirt was estimated
from five to one hundred feet. The company consisted of
ten in number and held ten thirty-foot claims and were
agreeable men, but their names are forgotten if I ever
knew them, for, as I have in a former chapter remarked,
at that time, in California, one might be intimate with
another for months and not know each other's names,
except as Tom or Jack or Bill. If one had a second name
it was generally merely descriptive, as, Feather River Bill, to
distinguish him from some other Bill. It was only by mere
accident that the full name and residence of an acquaintance was learned. Thus hundreds were forever lost to
their friends at home. But it was no fault of the miners,
for they would have been promptly advised by letter had
they been possessed of the names and address of distant
friends.

I worked in Gold Run some two months and left,
Powell remaining   I could not stand working in that

water, a large stream of which was running in the drive, and the drippings from the buckets at the shaft. All who worked below were wet through. The claim furnished water enough to wash out all the dirt they raised, which was no small amount, for they kept their long tom running night and day. Working was by shifts of eight hours each. I have stopped in a drive until I was obliged to crawl out on my belly, shoving my tools ahead of me, on account of twisting or skewing of the boxing in the wet soil. I have known shafts twist half around and close up so a bucket could not pass up and down.

As I had come to California with lofty aspirations and not to wear out my old clothes, as many pretended they did, I became dissatisfied with working for wages, and concluded to join a company to tunnel one of the Kiote hills to which I have before alluded. Some of the old Kiote diggings had become wet and consequently were opened at great labor and expense, and tunneling was the next process to be resorted to. Lessen's tunnel had already been started in the ravine below the hill, as it was then, for I don't know as there is any such hill there now, as I have not been there since 1852, but many will remember where it was then. That tunnel was put in to drain one side of the hill, and proved a good speculation. Our plan was to drain the other side by a longer tunnel, as the diggings went further into the hill the wetter they got. Sixteen persons constituted "The Enterprise Company." Among the names, so far as I can now remember them in full, were: L. O. Hart, Chester Babbet, H. G. Taft, Sherban Loveland, John Hunter, Richard Bean and C. D. Ferguson. There were also Coates, James and Johnston. All other names have passed out of memory. Our tunnel when completed was one thousand three hundred feet long, six feet in the clear, and solid timbered—some parts rock cut, some quicksand, and all expensive. Our tunnel was very wet, and a vast amount of quicksand was constantly flowing out. We worked five months in the enterprise, and when we had run into the hill where we expected to strike the lead of paying dirt, we found nothing but quicksand, and had to abandon it. Many years after, when I had become more experienced in mining, I could see where we had been deceived. A shaft was subsequently put down, not far distant in the same hill, by a party, one of them named Marlo, from Iowa, and had struck gold about sixty feet down on a false bottom, but went on through it to the main rock; the water, however, was so strong they could not work it and were compelled to abandon it, but a year afterwards it was discovered that our tunnel had drained the shaft, when they resumed work on the false bottom and found it to be very rich. Some years afterwards Powell worked it on wages, and I was informed that he had taken out as high as three thousand seven hundred dollars in a day. Mr. Lewis Taft also told me he had known it to yield from two dollars up to sixty to the tin dishfull, and all worked out by reason of the drainage of our tunnel. So in all probability we but just barely missed making our pile, and all for the want of a little more experience. Such was the fate of many other pioneer miners in California. The first do not always find reward in their enterprises; they only open up the way, and others who come along years afterwards, perhaps, reap the benefit of their hard toil and great expenditures.

After the Kiote hills had been opened and consequently drained, there came a scarcity of water, so that dirt had to be hauled to Deer creek, a mile or more, at great expense, which prevented many claims from paying. An enterprising man, Charles Marsh, an engineer, undertook to bring water by a ditch from Rock creek around Sugar Loaf mountain, a distance of five miles. It was regarded as a doubtful enterprise, but it succeeded. The creek, however, was small and the supply was not ample, but it was the beginning of what afterwards proved a great boom to Nevada City. Marsh was the pioneer of the supply for the diggings round about. He made a large reservoir to hold the water nights and Sundays, selling it out at the rate of an ounce of gold a day to the first user, to the next below, half an ounce, to those lower down a further reduction, when at last it found its way into Deer creek.

William M. Stewart, since United States senator for the state of Nevada, early had his eye open to business. Many laughed when he first engaged in it. It was putting in a long line of sluice-boxes running down the gully some three or four hundred feet, letting in all the tailings and water that run from the miners' toms. He kept a man on them constantly through the day with a sluicing fork, stirring up the dirt and keeping it loose. On Sundays, when the miners were not working, he cleaned out his boxes—with

what result none ever knew, except those interested, and
they kept it to themselves. I can now see that it must
have contributed largely to his fortune, for much of the
dirt was not half washed as it ran out of the various
toms of the miners and found its way into the future senator's sluice-boxes. At any rate, it doubtless paid him
better than running for the office of sheriff at the first
county election in Nevada in which he was badly beaten,
notwithstanding his generous contributions to the expenses of his campaign. He was not, however, an unpop-
ular man.

The success of Marsh's enterprise awakened others.
Two large companies were soon formed, and two more
ditches were dug, this time up Deer creek. More water
was needed, and there was no lack of spirit in Nevada
City. Only let the people see there was a want of some
improvement and the least prospect that the scheme
would pay, and money was plenty for it. Rock creek
ditch had demonstrated the practicability and profit of
such works. There were plenty of surface diggings that
would pay if water could be brought from Deer creek,
which was an ample stream to supply the wants of all.
The two ditches were built in an incredibly short time.
Competition brought water rents down so that surface
diggings would pay, miners make good wages and yet
the companies good dividends. The benefit was alike to
the miners and the public.

About the middle of 1851 Nevada City was startled by
a "midnight cry" from Grass Valley. It was the quartz
gold discovery, reputed to be wonderfully rich, but difficult

SACRAMENTO CITY, CALIFORNIA—AS IT WAS IN THE YEAR 1850.

to work, though men were making good wages pounding it with mortar and pestle. Soon it was seen that some process must be devised to get the gold out easier and faster. Judge Walsh and a Mr. Collins were the pioneers in quartz mills. It was in such a mill, some years later, that Mark Twain tells of his first job. He says he hired out at one hundred dollars a month to feed the stamps, and after working a month to their entire satisfaction they wanted to keep him on at the same wages. He offered to remain at five hundred dollars a month, but the indignant proprietors ordered him off the premises, and he was afterwards sorry he did not say a thousand, as they would have given it as readily as they would five hundred. I differ from Mr. Twain in my notion of the value of a month's services then and there, for I would not be hired to tend and feed such a machine for a thousand dollars a month. It was four head of stamps with wooden shanks, and the most it could do was to pound out two tons of quartz a day. Job was reputed a patient man, but he never tended a quartz mill like the first one in Grass Valley, and had his miserable comforters offered him a like situation, he would, or ought to have been requested to retire. Had the grand old patriarch worked a month in such a quartz mill, the record of his noble and patient character would never have come down to our time.

About this time the Bunker Hill Quartz Mining company was organized in Nevada City, but I did not take any stock in it for the reason, principally, that old Rigby was to be the manager of it, and I could take no stock in him or in anything he had anything to do with. A Dr.

Rodgers expected to astonish the world with his quartz smelting process. The company went to great expense in building a furnace, putting in a large water-wheel, rollers to crush the quartz, purchasing thousands of cords of wood for charcoal and constructing large fans to blow the fires of the furnace and puff to eternity the fame of Dr. Rodgers. Everything being prepared, all there would be to do would be to put in the charcoal, then the quartz on top, light the fire, put the fans in motion, then run off the gold in the bottom of the furnace, thus already smelted, into bars ready for coining. Some facetious wags suggested the propriety of attaching a mint to the works and coining the gold then and there to save expense of transportation to Philadelphia and back. The process, however, proved a dead failure, and in its results it was for that time and place a miniature South Sea bubble, for not only did capitalists, who generally subscribed to promote the enterprise, lose their entire investment, but many a poor fellow lost his whole summer's wages, besides being in debt for his board at twelve dollars a week. Rigby and Rodgers, the manager and projector, were enabled, through the handling of the stockholders' money, to make themselves whole. In this respect they were, indeed, both skillful "managers."

A San Francisco company started another crushing process, at the head of Wood's ravine, under the management of one Colonel Doan. This, also, proved a failure at first, but I do not know how it turned out in the end, though for the early history of quartz mining I think it was really a good plant. Colonel Doan had the regard and sympathy of all who knew him. Wood's ravine took a good start at the beginning of the quartz excitement. Two large hotels, or boarding-houses, were built there, one by Beauclerc, James and Butch, the second by Mr. and Mrs. Coates. We had long been tired of boarding ourselves, and now boarded with Coates at twelve dollars a week. Coates worked at mining and Mrs. Coates ran the boarding-house. He had been very successful in mining, and had made considerable money, and knew how to keep it. That faculty was so strong in him that it developed into very disagreeable penuriousness; besides, he was the most jealous man I ever saw. No person could speak to his wife but his suspicions were aroused. She was an active, enterprising and industrious woman, and popular for her kindness of heart and agreeable manners towards all. No more upright and honest woman ever came to California than Mrs. Coates. His jealousy was simply the outcome of constitutional meanness. Seeing his miserable disposition towards the noble woman, some of the boys mischievously put their heads together to keep him constantly in hot water. He had occasion to go to Sacramento, and for a change and rest she wanted to go with him, but he was too stingy to incur the increased expense, but took her over to Rock Creek to visit Mrs. Scott while he was gone. The boys were determined to get Mrs. Coates back home just to torment her disagreeable lord and master, but of their purpose and scheme Mrs. Coates was perfectly innocent. They had a little girl and boy of seven and five years old. Johnny was a bright little fellow, and the pet of his mother and all her

friends. Being put to their wits ends for a plausible
excuse for sending for Mrs. Coates, they finally had to
resort to the following scheme: There was an old quack
doctor in the place, always full of whiskey, and they
bribed him to give the boy just a little gentle emetic, and
as it commenced to operate they started a man off with
two horses, riding one and leading the other for Mrs.
Coates, and in less than an hour she was back again
among us. Johnnie's emetic had worked to a charm, and
he was out at play. She was greatly relieved to find the
dear boy in perfect health. Mrs. Coates remained at
home until her husband's return.

The other house ran a store as well, and James used, to
be on the road freighting to and from Sacramento. He
had four mule teams, and getting sick hired me to go two
trips with his other man. The first trip I made, as we
struck the Sacramento flats, a man passed me on horseback
under full gallop, the other teamster being ahead of me
an hour's distance. Not long afterwards I discovered
something like a bit of red ribbon sticking up through the
sand, apparently about five inches long. I stopped the
mules, got off, and to my great surprise found it to be a
bag of gold dust, of about eight pounds in weight. I
put it in the side box and went on. Presently I saw the
same man that had passed me about an hour before coming back. He asked the driver ahead of me if he had
picked up anything. He told him he had not, and of
course I being so far in his rear, he did not know that I had.
The man was very much excited as he confusedly asked
me if I had picked up anything? I asked him what he

had lost? He began to cry and said he had lost every
cent he was worth. "What was it?" said I. "A bag of
gold, all I am worth in the world, except my horse and
saddle," said he. I went to the side box, took out the
bag and asked him if that was it? "O yes," said he, and
seizing hold of the bag of gold immediately rode off, not
even so much as thanking me. I don't know whether the
fellow was too ignorant to be civil, or whether it was because he was so excited he did not know what he was
doing; I judge the latter, or at any rate I am willing to
give him the benefit of the doubt.

The next trip I made with a little loss myself. I was so
ashamed of it that I tried to keep it from the boys, for
they were always running me about my carelessness.
Upon leaving the Quartzville hotel, I stopped at Coates'
to take on a box, and a passenger who was going down
with me on his way home to the states. I helped him on
and put his box in the wagon and started, not stopping
until we reached Rough and Ready, where we watered
the mules and went in to water ourselves. I was humil-
iated when I found I had not a cent to pay the score with.
I went out to the wagon, but my coat was not there,
neither did I have the slightest idea where it was. The
other driver had money enough to pay the bill and so we
went on, and by the time we returned to Quartzville,
which was some eight days later, I had forgotten that
I had lost a coat. While we were at supper some person
spoke about someone having lost some gold and that
put me in mind of my coat. I then inquired of the land-
lord if anyone had seen a coat I wore when I was there

before. They all declared I wore it away, at any rate no
one had seen it. After supper I went up to Mrs. Coates',
and as no one had seen it there I gave it up as lost, but
just then the little girl spoke up and said Johnnie was cutting the buttons off a coat he found in the road yesterday.
We took a light and went into the little boy's room, and
sure enough there was my coat with all the buttons cut
off. I put my hand into the side pocket and pulled out a
purse containing about three hundred dollars. It had
lain in the road, and men and teams had traveled over it
for eight days, when Johnnie Coates picked it up to get the
buttons, and by that lucky circumstance my money was
saved. I tried to keep it a secret, but somehow the boys
got hold of it and there was no end of the chaffing I had
to submit to.

From teamster I found advancement in accepting the
position of chief cook at the Quartzville hotel where I
remained some four months at a salary of one hundred
and twenty-five dollars a month. As there was but one
cook at that hotel I cannot be overstating the truth when
I claim that I was chief. If possibly I am in error touching my rank, I cannot be regarding my salary, for it is
indelibly stamped upon my memory that Messrs. Beauclerc & Co. never paid the same, nor any part of two
hundred dollars money loaned them. I merely mention
this trifle, thinking possibly it may have slipped their
memory and that should they still remain this side of
Jŏrdan and be reminded thereof by reading this book,
they might be anxious to remit to me by draft. I shall
be generously disposed to waive the matter of thirty

years interest and give a receipt in full for the original sum.

It was in 1851, I think, when one morning in March we set out for the city, and on our way were surprised to see burnt pieces of calico strewed along the road, and even burnt shingles. Arriving at Nevada City we found the whole of Main street in ashes. The fire had broken out in Barker's gambling house, and spread so rapidly that in less than twenty minutes the whole street was one sheet of flame, and in an hour it was in ashes. Three of the finest buildings of the city were on this street. Scott's Empire, one of the most costly structures, had been opened but three nights when it was swooped up by the flames in an hour. The very next day by ten o'clock one could hardly get through the street for the men and teams clearing away, unloading lumber, and making ready for new buildings, and in a few weeks a stranger coming to the city would hardly know there had been a fire. Such were the enterprising spirits Nevada City was made up of in the golden days of '51. Moreover, those that did not suffer by the fire contributed generously to those who lost their all, and I don't know of a single instance where a man had lost even his last dollar but he could obtain credit to go right on and build up again. So we not only had enterprise in Nevada City, but generosity combined. The same has been my experience in whatever part of the world I have been. Enterprise and liberality go hand in hand.

Considering there was no public law in the territory until Nevada City was nearly two years old, I think one would have to travel far to find a more law-abiding people. There were but very few cases tried before Judge Lynch, only three cases of shooting, and those poor shots, only one man being killed, and only one case under the code of honor. The first shooting case occurred in Barker's gambling house, although the quarrel had been elsewhere. The affair was between two doctors, rivals for notoriety if not practice also, whose names I have forgottn. As they met, one pulled out a pistol and told the other to draw He threw up his hands and said he was not armed. Whereupon, the first pulled out another pistol and handed it to him, and in less than half a minute the house was clear of people—all that could get out. I was one of the unfortunate that could not get out, and took refuge behind the counter and a fifty gallon beer barrel. It was a close range struggle—pop, pop, and then a suspension for a few seconds, when I would stick my head up from behind the barrel to see if it was all over; then it would be pop, pop, and down would go my head again behind the friendly beer cask. At last each had discharged his five shots and what seemed very remarkable, neither was hurt. After it was all over they shook hands and drank together at the bar. The whole affair was a farce. It was simply a case of two mentally diseased doctors administering to each other bread pills, instead of good honest lead which would have cured both at that short range. The crowd only had been frightened, and as for myself, I never had any love for powder smoke under such circumstances, especially when I had reason to suppose there was a lead ball on top of the powder.

The next shooting case was that of Brown, a gambler, and Smith, a miner, which occurred in the Empire gambling house and grew out of a political dispute involving the abolition question. Smith used very abusive language which Brown put up with for a long time, but the more he forbore the more abuse Smith seemed disposed to heap upon him. Finally he told Smith to go away, whereupon Smith struck him. Smith was a stalwart six-footer, while Brown was a small man and no match for him. No sooner than he received the blow he drew his pistol and fired, the ball going through Smith's lungs. He fell and bled profusely. Of course the cry went out that a gambler had shot a miner and ropes were immediately in the hands of the multitude, they demanding that the wretch be hung, though not yet knowing the circumstances. The cooler ones, however, came in time to get Brown out of the way of the excited crowd, called a court and jury and tried the case, the hearing of evidence occupying two hours, when the jury returned a verdict of self-defense, and Brown was discharged. Smith had a pretty loud call, but by virtue of a strong constitution he lived. He was proved to be the aggressor, and the result was a lesson by which he profited by improved manners thereafter. Brown paid his doctor's bill and all his expense while he was laid up. Such was the gambler's style of doing things in the early days.

The last case of shooting happened in Kiota street the day of the first election. A man called Hayes, said to have come there from Cincinnati, and having the reputation of being a very mean and quarrelsome person, had a quarrel with a miner that morning over a pile of wash dirt, and had threatened to shoot the miner the next time he met him. His character was so well known that everyone regarded him as very likely to keep his promise in this respect if in no other, for he was entirely destitute of principle, and no little anxiety was felt for the miner, who was an old man and had a son about eighteen. When the son heard of Hayes' threat against his father, he walked into Bowers' express office, bought one of Colt's six-inch revolvers, loaded it without saying a word, walked up Main street, and when he turned up Kiota street he met Hayes and shot him in his tracks. There was, of course, another excitement, but it only lasted a few minutes, for as soon as anyone heard that it was old Hayes that was killed, that was enough; the universal expression was, "Served him right." The boy had a trial that lasted about an hour, and the verdict was, "justifiable homicide."

There was comparatively little thieving in and about Nevada City for so many people—perhaps from twelve to fifteen thousand—the principal case being that of a matter of three thousand dollars stolen from Napper's bakery shop. After a little his clerk was suspected and eventually acknowledged the theft. Two other young men had planned the robbery and the clerk had helped to carry it out. About half the money was recovered; the balance had been spent at the gambling table. The three were convicted and sentenced to receive thirty-five lashes each. Mr. Napper paid Butcher Bill five hundred dollars for administering the punishment. All felt the justice of the punishment, but everyone looked with contempt on the man that would whip another for pay. Had he volunteered to execute the law, or had Mr. Napper himself laid on the lashes, it would have been deemed the proper thing. From that moment Butcher Bill dropped to the lowest round of the social ladder, even to that of the thieves themselves.

At Rough and Ready an Indian was hung for the killing of a young man who was out looking for his uncle's horses. He had been found dead, pierced with arrows and mangled with a tomahawk. No one had witnessed it or knew the murderer, so the tribe was applied to for the surrender of the guilty Indian. They demurred at first, but were informed that if they did not comply the whole tribe would be held for the murder. At last they promised to do so as soon as they could find him, for he had become frightened and had hid himself. In a few days they found him, brought him in and surrendered him. Finding proof enough among the Indians themselves that he was guilty, hanging was next in order. Loveland, Taft and myself went down to witness the execution. The tribe did not arrive with the culprit till evening, so we had to lay over. In the meantime, the authorities had another little judgment to execute upon a Chilian who had broken into a store and had been caught in the act and had been adjudged to receive a certain number of lashes. As there was now territorial law, the culprit was in the care of the constable awaiting execution of the sentence—the expense of which would be a charge upon the county—so, as a matter of economy, while waiting for the murderer to be brought in, they thought it advisable to administer the lashes to the Chilian robber and save the county the expense. The constable wanted to make his fees and declined to give up the prisoner, so they kicked down the door and took him to a tree back of the jail and tied him. A doctor was present to decide how much the culprit could endure. A man was selected from the crowd to wield the lash. He received twenty-five stripes when the doctor ordered a stop. The blows occupied about one minute. As he was untied he fainted and fell; the doctor revived him with brandy and water, when he was given twelve hours to leave the district, with notice that if he returned he would be hung.

The Indians arrived in town about dark with the prisoner, Indian Dick by name, or as he was called. He was well known in the town as a bad fellow, and it was proved that he had enticed the young man out under the pretense that he had seen the horses. What he killed him for, perhaps was not very clear, but most likely for some trifle he had that the redskin fancied. The trial began in the evening and lasted till morning. Boyer, the Indian agent, was appointed interpreter. Verdict, "guilty." The judge, who had been up all night, went to bed as soon as the case had been submitted to the jury. The prisoner was guarded by the murdered man's uncle, a six-foot two-inch man, who stood sentry with a rifle nearly as long as himself. When the verdict was brought in, the judge was sent for to pronounce sentence. The uncle had been asked to go for the judge, but he declined to leave the prisoner, saying his post was by the Indian and there he should remain as long as the prisoner lived, which was not much longer.

Soon the messenger to the judge returned with the sentence
in writing that Indian Dick be hanged by the neck until
dead, but in the sleepy condition of the judge he omitted to
mention any time or place of execution. But such a little
technical or informal matter was of the least consequence,
for the crowd soon fixed time and place. The time was
instanter, the place the first tree. The convict was then
brought out, a dry goods box was placed under a limb of
the tree with a barrel on it, upon which Dick was placed
with his hands tied and his eyes blindfolded. By this time
someone had climbed the tree and fastened the rope. The
noose was adjusted to the murderer's neck, and the next
instant the barrel was knocked out and Dick was kicking
right and left, for they had forgotten to tie his legs. Some
twenty Indians were witnesses of the performance, laughing and seeming to enjoy it. I was in hopes the Indian
would attempt to escape, as I wanted to see the old uncle
drop him with that long rifle. I knew it would have done
the old man's heart more good to have shot him than to
have seen him hung. As soon as all was over the uncle
turned and walked out of town without speaking a word.
And now I will say right here that I would never witness
the like again, either of flogging or hanging, for idle curiosity.

The single duel with which Nevada City was credited,
as early as the spring of 1852, the time I left, was between
one Jim Lundy, son of the proprietor of Lundy's Lane,
famed as the battle-field of the War of 1812, and Charles
Dibble, then recently an officer of the Pacific mail line of
steamers. Jim was a noted duelist, this being, it was

said, his seventh duel. Dibble was a young man some-what addicted to drink, and having been discharged from the Pacific mail service, he came to Nevada City, where he got into some altercation with Lundy and challenged him. Lundy tried every means to prevent the meeting, but to no avail. He was a dead shot and no coward. The night before the meeting he shot the wick off a candle to convince Dibble of the danger he was liable to, but to no purpose. The meeting came off and Dibble was shot dead. One General Morehead acted as second for Dibble, but the name of Lundy's second I have forgotten. The authorities took the matter up, arrested, tried and fined the surviving principal and the seconds.

There was, in fact, another duel in Nevada City, but as it was irregular and wholly outside the code of honor, through the conduct of the seconds, it does not count in the record of dead shooting. Two old down-easters from Maine were rival musical artists, one a fiddler, the other a vocalist, and both were slightly addicted to drinking sprees, and when in the spirit they could not harmonize. They were known as old Wentworth and old Dan. On one occasion Dan was sawing away at his cat-gut when Wentworth considered himself entitled to the floor for a song, and being disturbed thereby, told Dan to stop that squealing thing. Dan felt insulted and demanded to know if he pretended his vocal ability to be equal to his instru-mental skill. Words multiplied words till their passions were thoroughly aroused, when nothing could wipe out the mutual insults but pistols and coffee, or rather, whiskey. A meeting was arranged; Hart and Hunter were seconds;

weapons, pistols; time and place, immediately, in rear of
the Quartz hotel. Before going, Wentworth proposed to
Dan to have one more drink together, as it was probably
the last on earth to one or the other. Dan assented, saying he knew very well which one was taking his last
drink. The principals were then placed, each taking his
stand as coolly as he ever stepped up to the bar for a
drink. The pistols were handed them; the word was
given and both fired. Wentworth fell covered with blood.
Dan approached and looked upon his bleeding victim, and
in maudlin utterances, said: "Poor f-feller, he wa'n't
f-fit to die." This was too much for the bleeding and
dying man, and he suddenly revived and jumped up and
demanded, "Who wa'n't fit to die?" He would let him,
Dan, know he *was* fit to die, although they had differed in
theology. Upon Dan's discovery that his antagonist was
not dead or dying, he was greatly pleased; took him by
the hand and rejoiced in the prospect of another drink
together. The fact was, the sportive boys had loaded one
pistol with powder only, and the other with a cartridge of
currant jelly—hence the blood

After the emigration of 1851 Nevada City was graced
by the presence of the fair sex numerously, who lent a
charm to the place we had never anticipated. The winter
following was a season of gayety, no end of balls and
social parties. In fact, the increased number of good
families of wives and daughters greatly improved the
social aspect of the town. The theatre greatly improved
and became a popular place of amusement with a higher
order of plays and actors. It was no longer the Nevada

City of '49 and '50. Fire-works were displayed both
magnificent and expensive, and proved remunerative to
the promoters of such entertainments, although the price
of admittance was only three dollars, barely the price of
three pounds of flour to the early immigrant. Three
thousand attended the first night, and the audience did
not diminish for several successive nights. The old Mexican bull-fighting was experimented in, but was not
patronized by people from the states, who found no pleasure in cruelty to animals, and it died out, though great
expense had been incurred in building a large amphitheatre.
The modes of fighting are various; sometimes a man on
foot, sometimes on horseback, and sometimes a Mexican
woman will exhibit her prowess and skill. The bull is let
into the arena after having been starved and kept in a
dark pen and every means used to torment him to get
him into a rage. When he first enters the arena he is
allowed to stand a few minutes and gaze at the crowd,
which he does, but they being of course out of his reach, he
looks around as if in search of something to vent his spite
upon. At this moment his antagonist appears, bearing in
one hand a rosette, in the other a red shawl, which he shakes
at him. The bull at once makes a dash at the shawl and
the party steps aside, and as the bull passes he hooks
the rosette into the animal's shoulder. This is painful
and crazes him so that he immediately turns for another
attack upon the flaunted red cloth, and passing again, in
like manner receives another rosette in the opposite
shoulder. This is sometimes repeated until the animal is
fully ornamented with rosettes, when the bull walks off

to one side to rest and contemplate the state of affairs, and the person also retires behind a screen and 'takes a rest. Then he appears with a long sabre or knife and again shakes the red flag, when the ferocity of the animal is increased and he makes another plunge at his assailant, who, after playing him as before, finally puts the sabre to the hilt into the bull's neck, near the shoulder; the blood spurts, and the poor animal walks to the other side of the ring, staggers for a few minutes, and then falls upon his side to rise no more. So thoroughly brutal and debasing is this relic of Spanish and Mexican barbarism, that I have even felt a regret that the bull did not survive the ordeal instead of the man. The bear-baiting and bull-fight are barbarous entertainments introduced from Mexico, and are alike both cruel to animals and debasing to human nature, and I forbear to further repeat their details.

While attending one of these barbarous Sunday exhibitions, someone tapped me on the shoulder. I turned to see who it was, and judge of my surprise to find it Martin M. Costler, my old friend and companion, who had crossed the plains with John See and myself. I never was more surprised in my life, especially to meet him at a bull-fight, and that too on Sunday, for he was a very religious man when he left the states, and, in fact, while crossing the plains. The gladness of our meeting was mutual. The only difficulty we ever had resulted from his efforts to correct my bad French, which, I am sorry to say, I sometimes expressed a little too emphatically when things went wrong. Of course he went home with me and we had a

long talk, fought over again all our battles with the Indians and told each other all our adventures since we parted
on Feather river two years before. He had been back to
Long's Bar to find me, hearing that See had gone home;
and not getting any tidings of me, concluded I had gone
with him. He had been to every digging in the country
in search of me. When we parted, two years before, he
went to Sacramento to work at his trade. Then there
came a rush for Redding's Bluffs and he went up there,
and then to some other place, and so on till he had boxed
the compass of all the diggings in the country, just
stopping in one place long enough to make sufficient money
to carry him to another. So it was with thousands that
went to California, first and last, and so it is in every place,
many are perpetually on the move. He staid with us a
while, got work at his trade and seemed content, that is,
for him, for he was always a little dissatisfied with the
world. He was, however, a very good fellow and liked
by all.

The Indians around Nevada were known as the South
Yuba tribe, and generally very quiet. The only murder I
heard of their committing was the one already related.
They were rather hard at driving a bargain. If they
bought anything they would pull out a little parcel of
gold, about a pennyweight at first; tell them that was
not enough, they would pull out as much more, which still
not being enough, they would say, "Got no more." Put
the article back on the shelf, they would produce another
parcel, and if they then got the article, they would stand
around till they saw something else they wanted, and

then they would repeat the same higgling process. Only one of a dozen would trade at a time; the others would look on, and if one got the same article a little cheaper, or for a little less quantity of gold, then there would be a great fuss to get the balance back. Their custom was hardly worth having; it was too much trouble to deal with them, the trouble of waiting on them being in excess of the value of their trade. Some were very good help about a hotel or a boarding-house. I remember Jim, at the Quartz hotel, a smart, gay fellow who worked there four months, got himself a good suit of clothes, bought a cheap Mexican pony, saddle and bridle, and one day went down to Bover's, among his tribe, to see his wives, as he said, but it was more to show his clothes and other evidences of his high civilized state, and to gamble, for they are all inveterate gamblers. About twelve o'clock, the next night, I heard a noise at the back door as of someone trying to get in, and went and opened the door. There stood Jim without a stitch of clothes on. He had gambled off all— clothes, horse and one of his wives, for he had two. The Indians believe in a plurality of wives, but two is generally the limit of such luxury, their financial resources not enabling them to attain unto the glories of Solomon.

Their mode of gambling is after this manner: Each takes a given number of sticks, a little longer than a common match, and sitting on the ground, facing each other, one takes three of the sticks in his hand and commences to go through a variety of motions, changing the sticks at the same time, the other watching him. After awhile he stops and the other guesses which hand they are in.

If he guesses right, he takes one of his opponent's sticks over to his pile, if wrong, he puts one of his over to the other's pile, and so on until one or the other has won all his opponent's sticks. That ends the game. The stakes are won by the lucky Indian, who gets an increase of estate and often an extra wife. They get very excited in gambling and will seldom give up as long as they have anything to wager, even to their wives, which last species of Indian property they affectionately reserve as the last thing to part with. Jim had got cleaned out and came back satisfied. We got him an old suit of clothes and he went to work as if he had lost nothing, at least to all appearances, though no one can tell whether an Indian is satisfied or not. They have what they call caroboreys, or fandangoes—a dance and a feast; the latter is a kind of soup made of dried acorns pounded to a flour and then stirred in cold water. When prepared, all sit around and each dips his forefinger in and licks off the soup. The one who gets the most dips gets the most soup. It pleases them much to have the whites join them in their finger-licking feast. The dancing is exclusively done by the men, ladies taking no part therein except as musicians. They sit off a little distance on the ground, some six or more composing the orchestra, each manipulating a sort of tambourine with two strings across it, with two beads on each string, which they beat with their fingers, at the same time keeping up a monotonous and dismal sort of song that makes a civilized man's flesh creep. The gentlemen's ball-room attire consists solely of a strip of calico fastened about the waist, some nine or ten inches in length, and the dancers, usually about twenty in number, dance in a circle. Their steps and movements would not be considered by our ladies and masters of our dancing schools as very graceful, but I can testify that, although they were barefooted, yet when they put their foot down one hears it, if not by the concussion, by the grunt the performer gives; that they keep excellent time— that is, I thought so, not judging by the music, but by the vibration of the ground for thirty feet around. This performance is kept up for about half an hour, when the whole party become thoroughly exhausted and the perspiration exudes from them as if a bucket of water had been dashed over them.

I never assisted at one of their funerals, but I have seen them in their mourning costume. The women take the most conspicuous part in inducting the deceased into the happy hunting ground. After the burial the women gather balsam from the fir tree and daub their hair and face with it, the dirt, of course, adhering, for they never wash themselves, and after a day or two their appearance is very repulsive. I never looked upon one of those creatures but my very flesh crawled with a feeling of disgust. If the Oriental philosophy of the transmigration of souls is correct, I pray that my soul may animate the body of bird or beast rather than that of a California Digger Indian, more especially one of the female branch.

CHAPTER XIII.

THERE had been great advancement in the method of
saving gold in the short space of time, about two
years, that I was in the country. At first the cradle was
used altogether for washing the dirt and separating the
gold therefrom, and quartz crushing was then unknown.
The first improvement was in using quicksilver, which
required a different cradle from that primitive one which I
have before described. The quicksilver cradle was fixed
upon rockers similar to the common gold cradle, only on a
larger scale and having a long drawer. The whole length
of the drawer was divided into six or eight little compart-
ments, made perfectly tight so as to hold quicksilver,
which is the most difficult to hold of all liquid substances.
The screen on top runs the whole length of the rocker,
punched with holes similar to the hopper of the early
cradle. The quicksilver is placed in equal portions in each

compartment of the drawer, when the rocker is put in a
slow rolling motion, the dirt having been put in at the
upper end; a gentle but steady stream is kept constantly
running in at the top where the dirt is put in, which gradually washes down and disappears through the sheet iron
screen and falls among the quicksilver, to which the gold
adheres, while the sand runs on with the water—the
coarser matter passing off over the screen. This process
was as short-lived as it was impracticable, except where the
gold was in loose sand and as fine as flour. A doctor at
Long's Bar, on Feather river, had a new-fangled machine
made of zinc, with partitions for the quicksilver as in the
above described rocker, which we concluded could be
worked at less expense than the former. We procured a
quantity of quicksilver at ten dollars a pound and commenced operations, but had run it but a brief time when
we discovered quicksilver running through the sand and
escaping. We stopped to look, not knowing but we had
discovered a quicksilver mine, and little thinking that ours
had eaten a hole through the zinc and was all gone, which
proved to be the fact. Neither of us knew it would eat
zinc. That put an end to our experiment with quicksilver,
after losing ten pounds and literally spoiling a rocker that
had cost the doctor forty dollars.

The next process that came into use was the long tom
which I have heretofore described. It was equal to a full
day's washing for two men, cleaning up in the evening
with about a tin dishful of dirt to pan off, when the gold
is all in the dish ready to dry and blow out the sand and
put it in the gold bag. Two men could wash in a long tom

some six loads of dirt in a day, and it was a great improvement over the old rocker, and would enable men to work diggings that yielded less gold to the load of dirt, and pay even better than richer dirt by the old cradle process.

Then came in vogue the sluice-box, which I have also before described. A long series of boxes, each some twelve feet long and one foot high and wide, fitted into each other and riffled on the bottom. Six men could shovel in all day, while one man with a sluicing fork stirred up the dirt to keep it from packing and forked out the large stones, and another at the end of the series of boxes shoveled away the tailings not already carried away by the water. This was deemed an improvement over the tom. It was said that dirt that would pay one cent to the tin dishful would amount to half an ounce a day under this process.

Afterwards came the process of ground sluicing, for surface dirt. A small ditch was cut on the side hill, just enough to make a course for the water, which, as it ran down, would wash the ground and loosen the lumps and the men would remove the large stone with their shovels. No one would believe the amount of ground six men could wash in a day who had not witnessed it. It was estimated that dirt that was a good strong color to the tin dishful would pay one ounce a day per man. We seldom cleaned up ground sluices oftener than once a week. This was done by uniting the various sluices, making one considerable stream, and placing boxes at the lower end to receive the entire week's wash, which, though reasonably successful, would be reduced to two or three dishfuls,

SAN FRANCISCO EARLY IN THE MINING ERA, 1850-51.

thus putting the week's work of from six to eight men into a pretty small compass.

Lastly was the advent of hydraulic washing which required great force of water, the stronger the better, which being run through hose they would commence in the face of a hill, sometimes washing away the whole hill before cleaning up, as it was called. Fortunes have been made by this method where the cradle and even the long tom men could not make their board. Before I left Nevada, early in 1852, there was a great deal of hydraulic mining being done between there and Rough and Ready, so that in two years mining had made great advancement since the days of the primitive rocker.

In the summer of 1851 the typhoid fever broke out in Nevada City, proving fatal to many people. Dr. Gardner, of whom I have already spoken, was himself a victim of the scourge. He was from Michigan and a young man, a good physician, and much lamented as a friend. George Raymond of Hiram, Portage county, Ohio, also died, besides a great many others whom I personally knew but whose names I can not at this moment recall. So it was in '49; you know him, he sickens and dies, and no one knows whence he came. His friends never get tidings of his fate, and not unlikely an aged mother is looking for his return even unto this day, still clinging to the hope that her boy, her youngest, who went to California in '49 or '50, will yet return to gladden her heart and receive her blessing. Many times have I been asked about an uncle—"My mother's brother, who went to California in '49 and we never heard from afterwards." They would tell his name and describe his looks, although the party giving the description was not born when the uncle left, but they had heard him described so many times by their mother or an aged grandmother that they really believed they knew how he looked. And the mother never gives up hope until she, poor soul, knows that her son is dead.

It was customary in the mining regions to go about on Sundays visiting one's neighbors, or to town to see the sights, so that that day was generally the most stirring day in the week. Loveland went to town to see a dentist, not knowing I had ever pulled a tooth. Taft staid at home, while I went to see Beauclerc, who was a great friend of ours. He told me he had just received a letter from an uncle of his in Australia; that gold had been discovered there by a man from California, by the name of Hargreaves, that was liable to become very rich diggings. I thought nothing more of it until I went home. Taft was cooking supper. I inquired for Loveland. "Oh," said he, "out star-gazing." I went out and found him standing a little distance from the cabin, his face turned starward, though I don't believe he was conscious of a star, for his mind seemed elsewhere. I asked him for his thoughts. He said Dr. Livermore, the dentist, who was formerly from Sidney, told him that he had just received a letter from Australia advising him that gold had been found there in quantity and richness surpassing anything then discovered in California. I then told him about Beauclerc's letter. "What do you say about our going?" said he. "All right," said I, "if you will go, I will." At that moment Taft called us to supper, and when we went in we told

Taft that we were going to Australia. "All right," said he, "if you go, I will go with you." We had not yet told him of the news, but did so immediately. We then talked over the whole matter, and finally, the same evening, all three of us started off to see Beauclerc. We found him as ourselves, but how to get away was a more difficult question. He had lately got married, and it was out of the question to take his wife with him on what might, after all, be but a wild goose chase. We left him, finally, with our own minds fully made up to go, but Beauclerc was to talk the matter over with his wife and determine what he would do. Taft and myself had Australia on the brain at fever heat. Loveland did not say much, but was, like the Irishman's parrot, thinking. We expected him to talk soon, and so he did. We sent Taft down to San Francisco to see about a ship. There was no more work to be done, for we suddenly discovered that our claim was worked out. Taft having gone, Loveland and I went about settling up our affairs. I had some money due me of which I collected a part and left the remainder of the claim with Hubbard & Hodge to collect and remit to my father and mother. They collected it promptly and paid it over to the person holding my father's order therefor, but my father never received but forty dollars out of the several hundred. My indignation has no limit when I contemplate the meanness of a man who will cheat or rob an old father of money sent him by his absent son to make his last days a little more comfortable. And I have sometimes thought that I could enjoy great exaltation of spirit if I could be absolutely assured of a hell—at least a department in Dante's 'Inferno' of about the temperature of a Turkish bath, fitted up expressly as the permanent residence in the spirit world of such as have wronged aged fathers and mothers. I have withheld the faithless man's name as I would avoid afflicting his family or relations, but hope if he still lives and these few lines should chance to meet his eye, he may be conscious of the great wrong and hereafter do work meet for repentance.

We now gathered together our mining tools and what provisions and bedding we did not take with us, locked up the hut and went into town and stayed the first night to be in time for the early morning stage for Sacramento, leaving the key of the hut with John Proctor, to be given to the first Farmington boy that should come. Proctor had been home since I left him in Marysville, and come back again to Nevada, and had gone into the milk business. The fare by coach to Sacramento, about seventy-five miles, was sixteen dollars. All kinds of fevers are more or less contagious, but I know of none that equals the gold-fever. It is fatal even among old acclimated California miners, hardly less than the Asiatic cholera in eastern cities. Loveland, Taft and myself were the first victims in Nevada City, but it spread rapidly, and others were soon as bad as ourselves. Martin Costler, who was always ready for a start for a new place, was ready then and there; Chester Babbet and L. O. Hart, from New York state; and Henry G. Nichols, from Twinsburg, Ohio. George Scott, of the Empire gambling house, and his wife took the fever, which carried them off "between two days." George was one of the most forgiving men I ever knew. He said he freely forgave his creditors and hoped they would be equally considerate towards him. Beauclerc had now made arrangements with Scott and wife at Rock Creek to keep his wife, so in the course of a week there were eleven in all "carried off," including Loveland, Taft and myself.

We arrived in Sacramento the same day we left Nevada City. Sacramento, even at that early day, was a city of some ten thousand inhabitants, handsomely laid out in square blocks, the streets running one way being indicated by numbers and the other way by letters. The buildings generally were of rather a temporary character, although some were very imposing to the eye. A great number on the back streets were of canvas. The city was situated near the junction of the American and Sacramento rivers. There was a large amount of business transacted there, as it was the principal outlet and depot to all the mountain towns and gold diggings. I met, while there, a man known to many in northern Ohio—David Brooks of Bristol, Trumbull county. He was in the auction business. We only remained here long enough to obtain the first steamer for San Francisco, where we arrived early the next morning, and were not long in finding Taft who had been there some two or three days. He informed us that there were two ships bound for Sidney, one the barque *Don Juan*, the other the ship *Constant*, but that neither would sail for two or three weeks. This was a great disappointment, but there was no remedy—what could not be cured must be endured—so we took up our quarters at the Commercial hotel, a very comfortable house on the Pacific wharf. In a day or two all the others afflicted with the Australian epidemic, arrived. While waiting for the ship, the only thing we could do was to go about the city sight-seeing.

San Francisco contained at that time, 1852, a population of about fifteen thousand. It had been twice completely destroyed by fire, but a stranger going into it as we did could not see a single sign of the destroying element. At least one-half of the city was built on piles, and underneath houses and streets the tide ebbed and flowed. The two principal streets leading down to the bay were Long and Pacific, and Montgomery was the principal cross street running through the town. There were already some large fire-proof buildings upon the latter street, banking houses and express offices, such as Adams & Co., Page, Bacon & Co.; in fact, Montgomery was to San Francisco what Wall street is to New York or Lombard, street is to London. Gambling palaces were plenty, and of humbler or lower ones there was no end. Long wharf was the chief quarters of high-toned aristocratic gambling. Cut-throat and land-shark gamblers were largely located on Pacific wharf, and many poor fools were there daily and nightly fleeced, in fact, robbed of their money. Served them right, I say, for if a man has no more sense than to visit such places and allow himself to be duped by swindlers, he is not fit to have money. Those located along Pacific wharf were not entitled to be designated as gamblers; they were simply cut-throats and thieves.

I will describe a game I witnessed up in the mines. It was easy enough for me to detect the cheat, although only a boy; yet I have seen plenty of full-grown men that would take the bait. It is played with dice, three in number, and is called the ABC game. There are six letters on each die, and sometimes all three letters turn up at the same time. If you have backed that letter the banker pays you three times the amount you have staked. To carry out the thieving principle the banker must have two accomplices. The banker sits at the middle of the table and throws the dice. One of his accomplices stands at a corner opposite, the second at the corner opposite the first and a little behind the banker. After the banker has thrown the dice, the accomplice opposite produces a a fifty gold piece or "slug" and wants change. The banker takes the gold piece and reaches over to count out the money, and while doing so accomplice number two pretends to lift the dice-box unbeknown to the banker, and if, perchance, there are three of a kind, he takes good care to let all the others standing around see it. He at once puts all the money he has on the letter that was seen under the dice-box, when his example is followed by one or more dupes. Then the banker says, "Are you all down? Bet your money, gentlemen, this bauk pays three to one." When all have put down their money he lifts the box, and to the disappointment of the dupes, the dice have been turned and not a letter that had been seen before is in sight, and the banker pockets their money. If they dare say a word in protest they are soon silenced. I don't wish to be understood that all games are conducted in this manner, or that this style of gaming is necessarily a swindle, for the ABC game fairly played is just as fair as any, though, of course, like all games, the percentage is largely in the banker's favor, but that the class of men who run this game were almost invariably swindlers and thieves. There were houses that would not tolerate swindling and were perfectly honorable in their dealings. Gambling was the pastime of the Pacific coast, and there were not many but indulged therein to some extent, as business men now in all cities resort to billiards and other games for temporary recreation. But the places where practices such as I have described were allowed, were dens of thieves.

Southwest of the city was old Wind-mill hill, and directly back was a chain of sand hills where a steam "paddy" was at work, which loaded a truck at every stroke. The sand was run down and filled into the bay; and now many acres of what was then the bay, constitute as many acres of solid land covered with buildings of four, five and six stories in height, and the sand removed to fill up the bay cleared away the great sand dunes, adding many acres of level land for the city's extension west, thus figuratively killing two birds with one stone. The rural surroundings of San Francisco I had no observation of at that time, though the Happy Valley was supposed to be as charming even then as the famed valley of Rasselas, prince of Abyssinia. It is some three miles out on the road to the old Spanish mission, which was established and the church erected some two hundred years ago, as I was informed, but cannot speak positively of my own knowledge, as it was considerably before my day.

The vigilance committee was still in force, but at the time they had very little to do. A short time before our ar-

rival, there had been a great excitement over the hanging of
Whitaker, McKensie and Stuart.   All three were convicts
from Van Diemen's Land.   The two first named were taken
from jail and hanged for murder and robbery.   The last
named was caught in the attempt to make away with a
small iron safe he had managed to remove from some office
near the docks, and had got it into a boat and was rowing
across the bay when he was caught, though not before he
threw the safe overboard.   He was brought ashore and
marched up to a warehouse, a rope was adjusted to his
neck, and he was run up on the pulley by which goods were
hoisted.   Captain Wakeman superintended the brief ceremonies.

While awaiting our ship's sailing, I made one trip across
the bay to Contra Costa, as it was then called, a distance
of some ten miles, in a sail-boat, and went out into the
country about three miles blackberrying.   When I came
back to the town of about a dozen houses I indulged in a
dish of clam chowder, the first and probably the last I
shall ever eat, if it is all like the clam chowder of Contra
Costa, which impressed upon my mind as lasting memory
of the place.   It was as obnoxious to my taste as the first
glass of beer I ever drank.   One hot day I saw people step-
ping up to the bar and calling for a glass of beer.   I saw
the white foam and it looked very tempting, and so I called
for one.   I had only tasted it when I would willingly have
given a dollar if someone had stepped up and drank it for
me, but I had called for it and was ashamed to leave it,
and so I had to worry it down.

At that time there were two lines of ocean steamers,

the Panama and the Central America. While I was there the *Winfield Scott* came in on her first trip—the largest passenger steamer that had ever come around the Horn. When Loveland and I first arrived in San Francisco and engaged lodgings in the hotel, we were told that the house was full, but if we had no objections to another room-mate, they could accommodate us—that he was one of the best of fellows. So we consented, provided the stranger would accept us. We were shown up and found that our roomer was not in, so we washed and breakfasted and then went out about the city. When we returned we went to our room. We found it full. Upon coming in our future mate introduced himself, and the rest of the company as his friends. He appeared to be very much of a gentleman, and played the violin like Ole Bull, which was enough to make us take to him at once. His name was James Hull, second officer of the Pacific mail steamer *Oregon*, which was then undergoing repairs at Benecia. The others were officers of other steamers then in port, either just arrived or about to leave. One was Darius Pollock, a rather young man to hold the office of second engineer, I thought, especially when I listened to his rattling conversation, and I remarked the same to Hull, who told me I would change my mind when I knew him better, and particularly if I should once see him on duty. Hull told me how Pollock came by his early promotion. He was coming up from Panama, Captain Knight, the head man of the Pacific mail line of steamers, being on board, when a little girl, playing on the hurricane deck, fell overboard, the steamer being under full way, some ten miles an hour. Pollock saw the child fall, and in an instant he was over after her, striking the water almost as soon as she did. They both went down out of sight, and those on board who witnessed the scene thought they would rise no more, so long were they under water. Presently, however, he appeared, holding up the little girl with one hand and with the other striking out for the steamer. It was stopped as soon as possible, boats were lowered, and they were both picked up and soon safe on board, the little girl only the worse for the wetting. Pollock immediately went down into the engine room as if nothing had happened. A purse was soon raised by the passengers to present to him as a testimonial of their gratitude for his heroic deed. He was called up to receive the purse, but to their surprise he declined it, saying he had only done his duty—that it was the duty of all men to save a life when they had the opportunity. Upon that Captain Knight stepped forward and complimented him upon having done his duty so nobly and so well, and said that he also had a duty to perform, and at once, then and there, publicly promoted him to the position of second engineer.

Pollock was a fearless man and sometimes a little reckless, but withal a good-hearted fellow. One day I rode out with him and some of the other boys to Happy Valley, and on our return, rather late in the evening, Pollock took a notion to call at the house of an acquaintance and rouse him out of bed. The door being locked, he commenced to rattle away at the latch to awaken his friend. Suddenly a head appeared at an upper window and demanded to know who was there. He did not answer, but rattled still more at the latch. "Go away," said the man at the window, "or I will shoot"—at the same time presenting a pistol—one of Allen's six-barrel pepper-boxes, as they were called, good for shooting around corners—and commenced to pop away at Pollock, who stood all the while with one arm akimbo, saying, "Look out, be careful with that d—d thing; you might hit somebody!" His voice and peculiarity of expression disclosed who he was, and the friend came down, unlocked the door and let us all in. The affair was considered a good joke, none of the party seeming to consider the danger of such careless shooting.

There was one Frank Beaubie whom we met in 'Frisco, that some alive and still sailing on the lakes may remember as commander of the Canadian steamer *London*. He was first mate of the mail steamer *Oregon*. I afterwards met a cousin of his in Australia. Benecia was the place up the bay where steamers underwent repairs, consequently it was a great rendezvous for the officers and crews when laid up. A party of us went up there one day, among whom was one Charlie Taylor. In the course of the evening Charlie imbibed so freely of the elixir of life that the boys had to put him to bed; but before leaving him they took all his clothes, even to his shirt. When he awoke in the morning, he found his clothes gone. The others were at breakfast, expecting every moment to be sent for by Charlie. Presently there was a commotion on the stairs and a jingling of a pair of Mexican spurs, and the waiters barring his way, telling him he could not come down in that condition. Looking in to see what was the matter, there stood Charlie in full costume of nature, decorated with a pair of Mexican spurs and a shirt collar. His

clothes were brought forth, and peace was restored between Charlie and the waiters. The whole three weeks we
were waiting in 'Frisco, our room was full of cheerful and
friendly persons, which was a great benefit to us who were
necessitated to kill time, being always ready to show us
every civility and attention. They were gentlemanly in
manners, young and full of fun, and able and willing to
bear their proportion of expenses. We were enabled through
them to see and know more of the city than otherwise we
could have seen and known, as they knew all the ropes,
as the saying is, and would let no stranger in their company be imposed upon.

The time was drawing near for our departure, and we
had all decided to take the *Don Juan*, a barque of some
three hundred tons register. She had been laid up in the
bay over two years, having, like many other vessels in the
early days of the gold rush to California, been deserted by
the whole crew and never been able to put to sea again.
The *Don Juan* had been purchased by Smith & Son, and
laid on for the Australian passenger trade. The fare was
$60. The captain that was to have sailed her was Tucker,
but upon pulling out into the stream, his creditors remembered him with such depth of feeling that, like Pharaoh,
their hearts were hardened, and they would not "let him
go." They got out an attachment for his body, and the
consequence was that after being ready to sail, our barque
had no captain. After some delay, Captain John Sears
took command. He was a young man of about twenty-
two years, every way competent to assume the responsi-
bilities of any ship that ever sailed the Pacific ocean.

Before leaving Nevada City, we had had letters from home telling us some more Farmington boys had started for California, and that we might expect them on the arrival of the steamer *North America*. Word came to 'Frisco that the steamer had been wrecked down on the coast off Acapulco, and the sailing ship *Northern Light* was sent down there to bring up the passengers. We had been on the lookout some days, hoping to see the boys before we sailed, and while we were anchored in the bay, waiting for our new captain, the *Northern Light* came inside the Golden Gate, passed us and dropped anchor. This put Loveland, Taft and myself into great excitement to see the boys from home. Upon inquiry, we found our ship would not sail till five o'clock the next morning, and that we could go if we were sure to be aboard again by that time. So we got a boat and went ashore and, to make sure of our return in time, hired the boatman to stop for us all the while, that there might be no default of reaching our ship in time. We had not gone two hundred yards up the wharf when I heard a voice say, "There is Charlie Ferguson. I know him." Sure enough, there were three of the boys from home, schoolmates, with whom I had played, swam Grand river, and changed works when our fathers had set us some little task to do, which we thought could not be done alone. And now, here on Pacific wharf in California, after years of absence and wandering, I met Milo Griffith, one of those boys, and all my boyhood recollections were revived. I was delighted to see them all, and our feelings were mutual.

They had been shipwrecked and had been compelled to

stay in Acapulco until their money was all gone, and had now been landed here with neither money nor friends, as they supposed, until they unexpectedly ran across us. They had two others with them, strangers to us, who were in the same predicament as our friends, and of course had to be provided for, as an old California miner never makes flesh of one and fish of another when the necessities of life are wanted. We gave the boys enough to pay their expenses up to their hut, told them to go to John Proctor for the key, take possession, and if they liked they could go into our claim and make wages, which, since my return, they have told me they did. We, of course, were up with them all night until about three o'clock, when we parted from them. By this time our boatman began to show signs of weariness, and so we entered the boat and pulled for the *Don Juan*, and were on deck a few minutes before she weighed anchor. Soon we were outside the Golden Gate, myself little thinking that thirty-one years would roll around before I should again set foot upon American soil; that before my return, the goddess of history would multiply her pages in recording the rise and fall of empires, the crumbling of thrones, the oscillation of France and Spain between a monarchy and a republic, the unification of Italy, civil war in the United States and the emancipation of the slave, the Suez canal, Sedan and the German empire, the rediscovery of the sources of the Nile, the Pacific railway, the electric light and the telephone—wondrous events of a single generation.

The Far Western Frontier

An Arno Press Collection

[Angel, Myron, editor]. **History of Nevada.** 1881.

Barnes, Demas. **From the Atlantic to the Pacific, Overland.** 1866.

Beadle, J[ohn] H[anson]. **The Undeveloped West; Or, Five Years in the Territories.** [1873].

Bidwell, John. **Echoes of the Past:** An Account of the First Emigrant Train to California. [1914].

Bowles, Samuel. **Our New West.** 1869.

Browne, J[ohn] Ross. **Adventures in the Apache Country.** 1871.

Browne, J[ohn] Ross. **Report of the Debates in the Convention of California, on the Formation of the State Constitution.** 1850.

Byers, W[illiam] N. and J[ohn] H. Kellom. **Hand Book to the Gold Fields of Nebraska and Kansas.** 1859.

Carvalho, S[olomon] N. **Incidents of Travel and Adventure in the Far West; with Col. Fremont's Last Expedition Across the Rocky Mountains.** 1857.

Clayton, William. **William Clayton's Journal.** 1921.

Cooke, P[hilip] St. G[eorge]. **Scenes and Adventures in the Army.** 1857.

Cornwallis, Kinahan. **The New El Dorado; Or, British Columbia.** 1858.

Davis, W[illiam] W. H. **El Gringo; Or, New Mexico and Her People.** 1857.

De Quille, Dan. (William Wright). **A History of the Comstock Silver Lode & Mines.** 1889.

Delano, A[lonzo]. **Life on the Plains and Among the Diggings;** Being Scenes and Adventures of an Overland Journey to California. 1854.

Ferguson, Charles D. **The Experiences of a Forty-niner in California.** (Originally published as *The Experiences of a Forty-niner During Thirty-four Years' Residence in California and Australia*). 1888.

Forbes, Alexander. **California:** A History of Upper and Lower California. 1839.

Fossett, Frank. **Colorado:** Its Gold and Silver Mines, Farms and Stock Ranges, and Health and Pleasure Resorts. 1879.

The Gold Mines of California: Two Guidebooks. 1973.

Gray, W[illiam] H[enry]. **A History of Oregon, 1792–1849.** 1870.

Green, Thomas J. **Journal of the Texian Expedition Against Mier.** 1845.

Henry, W[illiam] S[eaton]. **Campaign Sketches of the War with Mexico.** 1847.

[Hildreth, James]. **Dragoon Campaigns to the Rocky Mountains.** 1836.

Hines, Gustavus. **Oregon:** Its History, Condition and Prospects. 1851.

Holley, Mary Austin. **Texas:** Observations, Historical, Geographical and Descriptive. 1833.

Hollister, Ovando J[ames]. **The Mines of Colorado.** 1867.

Hughes, John T. **Doniphan's Expedition.** 1847.

Johnston, W[illiam] G. **Experiences of a Forty-niner.** 1892.

Jones, Anson. **Memoranda and Official Correspondence Relating to the Republic of Texas, Its History and Annexation.** 1859.

Kelly, William. **An Excursion to California Over the Prairie, Rocky Mountains, and Great Sierra Nevada.** 1851. 2 Volumes in 1.

Lee, D[aniel] and J[oseph] H. Frost. **Ten Years in Oregon.** 1844.

Macfie, Matthew. **Vancouver Island and British Columbia.** 1865.

Marsh, James B. **Four Years in the Rockies; Or, the Adventures of Isaac P. Rose.** 1884.

Mowry, Sylvester. **Arizona and Sonora:** The Geography, History, and Resources of the Silver Region of North America. 1864.

Mullan, John. **Miners and Travelers' Guide to Oregon, Washington, Idaho, Montana, Wyoming, and Colorado.** 1865.

Newell, C[hester]. **History of the Revolution in Texas.** 1838.

Parker, A[mos] A[ndrew]. **Trip to the West and Texas.** 1835.

Pattie, James O[hio]. **The Personal Narrative of James O. Pattie, of Kentucky.** 1831.

Rae, W[illiam] F[raser]. **Westward by Rail:** The New Route to the East. 1871.

Ryan, William Redmond. **Personal Adventures in Upper and Lower California, in 1848–9.** 1850/1851. 2 Volumes in 1.

Shaw, William. **Golden Dreams and Waking Realities:** Being the Adventures of a Gold-Seeker in California and the Pacific Islands. 1851.

Stuart, Granville. **Montana As It Is:** Being a General Description of its Resources. 1865.

Texas in 1840, Or the Emigrant's Guide to the New Republic. 1840.

Thornton, J. Quinn. **Oregon and California in 1848.** 1849. 2 Volumes in 1.

Upham, Samuel C. **Notes of a Voyage to California via Cape Horn, Together with Scenes in El Dorado, in the Years 1849–'50.** 1878.

Woods, Daniel B. **Sixteen Months at the Gold Diggings.** 1851.

Young, F[rank] G., editor. **The Correspondence and Journals of Captain Nathaniel J. Wyeth, 1831–6.** 1899.